FLEUR WOOD IS ONE OF AUSTRALIA'S LEADING
FASHION DESIGNERS. SHE HAS STORES AROUND
AUSTRALIA, ALONG WITH A LOYAL CLIENTELE IN
THE UNITED STATES AND EUROPE. HER BRAND HAS
BECOME SYNONYMOUS WITH BEAUTY AND STYLE.

SHE HAS ALWAYS HAD A PASSION FOR ENTERTAINING,
WHICH FINDS EXPRESSION IN HER FIRST BOOK:
FOOD, FASHION, FRIENDS.

FLEUR LIVES IN SYDNEY WITH HER HUSBAND
NICK AND THEIR LABRADOR SKIP.

**FOR NICK,
WHO LOVES FOOD MORE THAN FASHION
AND IS MY VERY BEST FRIEND**

LANTERN

an imprint of

PENGUIN BOOKS

food
fashion
friends
FLEUR WOOD

At home I have a kitchen shelf almost buckling under the weight of cookbooks, old and new, but I have always felt that one title was missing. Many are the times that I have reached for a book that would not only provide recipes for what to cook, but inspiration on how to put an entire menu together, from the canapes through to the dessert.

Things eventually came to a head when I awoke from a restless sleep early one Saturday morning to the daunting prospect of six friends arriving later that evening for supper. What should I serve as the entree? What could I cook as a complementary main? Oddly, it was my complete lack of inspiration early that morning that ultimately provided the inspiration for this book.

It was also born of a love of entertaining that I can trace back to my Sydney childhood. Some of my happiest and most abiding memories from that time are of watching my parents welcome friends into our suburban home. The gold-plate cutlery would come out. The fine china would also make a rare appearance. Dad would put on some Frank Sinatra or Elvis, while Mum would spike the ice cubes with gin. Back then, I would watch with wide-eyed wonder as Mum spent hours preparing the food – some curried snapper with a garnish of tinned pineapple, perhaps, or flambeed bananas. It all seemed very exotic at the time.

Just before the guests arrived, I would rifle through Mum's wardrobe, plucking out outfits for her to wear. Then I would stand peering up from the tiled bathroom floor as she styled her hair and put on her make-up, with some fabulously seventies flourishes. Late into the night, I would listen to laughter coming from the lounge room. Then, early the next morning, I would creep out of my bedroom, finish off the leftovers and go in search of any stray After Eights left scattered on the table. To my impressionable young mind, entertaining seemed glamorous, beautiful, fun – and the height of sophistication. It sparked my imagination even then.

My fascination with fashion grew from an early age, too. When an older sister took me down to the local newsagent and invited me to pick out something to read, I ignored the shelves of comic books and pointed a precocious finger in the direction of the latest issue of *Vogue*. I watched *Moonlighting* and *Dynasty*, out of a strange, pre-adolescent enthrallment with Cybil Shepherd's power-suits and Linda Evans' sequined eveningwear. At the age of eight, I decided to give myself the grand title of 'family fashion consultant', and found what I thought were willing clients in my elderly aunties.

From the suburbs of Sydney, the journey into the fashion industry took me on a strange and circuitous route. To the Himalayas in northern India, for a start, where I spent two years with the exiled Tibetan community in Dharamsala. Setting out in search of spiritual enlightenment, I soon found myself chanting with Tibetan monks in their mountain-top temples and chilling out on the beaches of Goa. I not only immersed myself in the mysticism of India. Its lavish colours, fabrics and crafts were also irresistible. So, returning to Sydney I was filled with a new sense of purpose: I would launch my own textile business, from which my fashion label grew.

Joining me on that meandering journey have been some wonderful, food-loving friends and relatives. Flatmates who were serious foodies. Generous parents who prided themselves on their hospitality. Colleagues in the fashion industry with refined tastes and exquisite style. Old pals, like the internationally acclaimed chef Matt Moran, who has turned cooking into an art form. A husband who works as a globe-trotting foreign correspondent and who considers himself a world authority on food – based not so much on his knowledge of local cuisines as an insatiable level of consumption.

introduction

So this book brings together three things I have come to cherish and hold dear: food, fashion and friends.

It sets out a variety of recipes, menus and styling suggestions for a range of meals and events: the quintessential dinner party, the relaxed weekend brunch, a kids' party, an elegant afternoon tea, a simple country picnic. Some are straightforward. Others are much more intricate and sophisticated: more 'happy to slave all day' than 'throw it quickly together'.

Likewise, the food ranges from the really simple to the really complicated. There are the scrummiest chocolate cookies, pork roasts and lobster sandwiches. Then there are recipes for souffles, meringue cakes and rabbit ballotine. There are new twists on old favourites, such as macaroni cheese and the good old fondue. I have also managed to prise out some of the secret recipes from my favourite restaurants, such as the panna cotta from Italian restaurant Vini, in Sydney's Surry Hills. You can decide whether to serve the suggested menus in their entirety or choose individual dishes to present on their own. To make the most of these delicious recipes, I encourage you to use seasonal, organic produce wherever possible. Not only is it better for you and the environment, it simply tastes better.

Just as the flavours and food come from all over the world, so, too, does the sense of fashion and style. There's inspiration from the flea markets of Paris to the vintage fairs of Manhattan; from the villages of rural England to the urban grunge of inner London; from the boutiques of Tokyo to the coastline and harbour of Sydney, which always draw me home.

The props have come from all over, as well: beautiful antiques, family hand-me-downs, sails from a shipyard, spray-painted backdrops, discarded milk crates and the occasional, bewildered cow.

Good food is best served with a great soundtrack. For that I have turned to my musical guru, Gary Sinclair, who always looks after the sound at my fashion shows. Again, there's everything from Pink Martini to The Velvet Underground, from Vivaldi to Massive Attack.

When it comes to entertaining, I would never claim to have all the answers. Far from it. There have been times in my kitchen when things have gone disastrously wrong, such as the night when the rice I was cooking stuck to the bottom of the pan and I tried to pass it off as smoked risotto – a recipe which, needless to say, did not make it into the book.

For all that, I hope that *Food, Fashion, Friends* will enthuse and inspire. This book, remember, grew from a gap on my kitchen shelf. I hope it will fill that vacant slot on yours.

Hot-House High Tea

INDULGENT AND SOPHISTICATED,
THIS HIGH-TEA MENU IS PERFECT
FOR A BRIDAL OR BABY SHOWER,
OR SIMPLY SPOILING YOUR
CLOSEST GIRLFRIENDS.

Pardon my dreamy nostalgia,

but I would have loved to have lived during an era when high tea was an everyday ritual rather than a special and occasional treat. Perhaps it is the feeling of decadence; perhaps it is the femininity of those dainty sandwiches; perhaps it is all of those cakes and sweets; perhaps it is the simple and innocent pleasure of drinking piping-hot tea from bone china.

For this high tea, we chose a lush, botanical setting: a glasshouse full of plants and greenery, with giant wicker chairs adding to the sense of extravagance and luxury. I guess you could call this a hot-house high tea, where the most exotic flowers of all were obviously the models themselves.

I love indulging my girlfriends with a menu I've made entirely from scratch, from simple butterfly sandwiches to show-stopping sponge cakes. However, when I have been working crazy hours and time is short, I have no problem ordering in a few items from my local bakery or gourmet deli. (This is where I admit to not making the macaroons for this shoot. They looked so pretty, I just had to have them.) But it is always far more satisfying serving – and eating – a cake that you have made yourself.

After a long afternoon of very ladylike behaviour, there was an obvious temptation to let loose with a food fight. But, as everybody knows, girls in glass houses should not throw scones . . .

Set the Scene

Styling

CANE PEACOCK CHAIRS,
    PAINTED IN PASTEL COLOURS
POTS OF FLOWERING ORCHIDS,
    FERNS AND PALMS
A CHINA TEA SET AND COCKTAIL GLASSES
ASSORTMENT OF CAKE STANDS AND PLATTERS
LACE DOILIES

Playlist

NOUVELLE VAGUE *Bande à Part*
VARIOUS ARTISTS *Hollywood, Mon Amour*
EMILIANA TORRINI *Me and Armini*
RICKIE LEE JONES *Naked Songs: Live & Acoustic*
VARIOUS ARTISTS *So Frenchy So Chic*

Menu

CITRUS TEA
PROSECCO WITH WATERMELON SORBET

.

Savoury Bites
LOBSTER SANDWICHES
PATE BUTTERFLIES
QUAIL EGG AND TRUFFLED MUSHROOM CHOUX PASTRIES

.

Sweet Treats
COCONUT ICE
CHEAT'S MILLE-FEUILLE WITH CHOCOLATE MOUSSE
LEMON CAKE WITH EARL GREY ICING
RHUBARB MERINGUE CAKE

.

Citrus Tea

Clean citrus tea – sipped from your best china, of course – is the perfect accompaniment to this decadent feast.

80 g (1 cup) black tea leaves
zest of 2 lemons
zest of 2 limes
zest of 1 orange

Combine the tea leaves and zest in a small bowl. Place the tea mixture in a large teapot and add boiling water.

Infuse the citrus tea for 2–3 minutes before pouring.

Serves 6

Coconut Ice

Such a pretty old-fashioned favourite loves a modern twist. Try adding rosewater to the pink coconut or replace the dark chocolate with white for an even sweeter treat.

320 g (2 cups) pure icing sugar
¼ teaspoon cream of tartar
1 × 395 g can sweetened condensed milk
320 g (3½ cups) desiccated coconut
6 drops pink food colouring
150 g good-quality dark chocolate, melted

Lightly grease a 30 cm × 20 cm slice tin and line with baking paper.

Sift the icing sugar and cream of tartar into a large bowl. Add the condensed milk and coconut, and stir well. Transfer half of the mixture to the prepared slice tin and press down, levelling well. Add the food colouring to the remaining mixture and stir to combine.

Pour the chocolate over the white coconut ice in the tin and use a spatula to spread evenly over the top. Carefully spread the pink coconut ice over the top of the chocolate and press down, levelling well. Refrigerate for 2 hours or until set.

To serve, turn out the coconut ice and cut into small squares.

Serves 8–10

Prosecco with Watermelon Sorbet

Sweet sorbet with a twist of lime works beautifully with the dry sparkling wine.

110 g (½ cup) caster sugar
360 g (2 cups) roughly chopped seedless watermelon
2 tablespoons lime juice
1 egg white
750 ml prosecco

Place the caster sugar and 250 ml (1 cup) of water in a saucepan and bring to the boil, stirring until the sugar dissolves. Reduce the heat and simmer for 5 minutes. Remove sugar syrup from the heat and allow to cool.

Place the sugar syrup, watermelon and lime juice in a food processor and blend for 1 minute. Transfer to a glass bowl and freeze for 1 hour.

Using an electric beater, whisk the sorbet until it breaks up, then return to the freezer for a further 30 minutes. Repeat this process twice more, whisking every 30 minutes.

Whisk the egg white in a clean glass bowl until soft peaks form. Using a metal spoon, stir through the watermelon mixture and then whisk with an electric beater until well combined. Cover tightly and freeze overnight.

To serve, spoon the sorbet into glasses and pour over the prosecco.

Serves 6

Lobster Sandwiches

Two simple sandwiches cut into gorgeous butterfly shapes. Lobster is an indulgent treat, but you'll find a little goes a long way in these delicate little bites.

250 g cooked lobster meat, finely chopped
1 bunch chives, finely chopped,
    plus extra to garnish
sea salt and cracked black pepper
40 g butter, softened
12 slices white bread

Lemon mayonnaise
1 egg yolk
1 teaspoon Dijon mustard
1 teaspoon lemon juice
250 ml (1 cup) light olive oil

For the lemon mayonnaise, place the yolk, mustard and lemon juice in a glass bowl and whisk until well combined. Slowly pour in the olive oil, continuing to whisk until thick and well combined.

Combine the lemon mayonnaise, lobster and chives in a bowl. Season with salt and pepper.

Butter the slices of bread. Add the lobster mix to half of the slices and top with the remaining bread.

To serve, cut the sandwiches into butterfly shapes using a butterfly-shaped cutter, and garnish with the extra chives.

Serves 6

Pate Butterflies

12 slices rye bread
220 g good-quality pate
2 tablespoons finely chopped parsley (optional)

Using a butterfly-shaped cutter, cut a butterfly from each piece of bread. Toast the butterflies under a hot grill for 2–3 minutes on each side or until golden.

Using a sharp knife, cut 6 of the butterflies in half (down the spine of the butterfly) and set aside – these will be the wings. Place a teaspoon of pate in the middle of each whole butterfly and stick a set of wings into the pate to sit at a 45-degree angle.

Sprinkle with parsley and add more pate to taste, if desired.

Serves 6

Quail Egg and Truffled Mushroom Choux Pastries

Making your own choux pastry can seem daunting, but it's an art worth mastering. I think it's actually a lot easier than some pastry chefs would have you believe.

6 quail eggs
40 g black caviar

Truffled mushroom
20 g butter
200 g button mushrooms, finely chopped
sea salt and cracked black pepper
1 black truffle, finely chopped

Choux pastry
60 g unsalted butter
pinch of salt
125 g plain flour, sifted
3 eggs

Preheat the oven to 180°C. Line a baking tray with baking paper.

For the choux pastry, combine the butter, salt and 180 ml (¾ cup) of water in a small–medium saucepan and bring to the boil. Remove from the heat and add the flour, stirring to combine. Return the pan to the heat and stir over medium for 3 minutes or until the mixture starts to come away from the sides of the pan.

Transfer the mixture to a deep bowl. Beat with an electric mixer, while adding the eggs one at a time. Spoon 12 heaped teaspoons of the choux mixture onto the prepared tray. Bake for 40 minutes or until golden. Transfer to a wire rack to cool.

Meanwhile, place the quail eggs in a saucepan and cover with water. Place over medium heat and simmer for 4 minutes or until the eggs are cooked and soft in the middle. Remove the eggs from the saucepan and allow to cool before peeling. Cut in half and set aside.

For the truffled mushroom, melt the butter in a frying pan over medium heat. Add the mushrooms and cook for 5–6 minutes or until softened. Season with salt and pepper. Remove from the heat and stir through the truffle.

To serve, slice the top off each pastry and spoon in a teaspoon of the truffled mushroom. Add half a quail egg, garnish with caviar and top with the pastry lid.

Makes 12

Cheat's Mille-feuille with Chocolate Mousse

If the choux pastry seems too complicated, try this instead. If you're feeling adventurous, experiment with different fillings: custard, cream or strawberry mousse are all delicious alternatives.

3 sheets ready-rolled puff pastry
2 tablespoons caster sugar
1 × 300 g tub good-quality chocolate mousse
icing sugar, for dusting

Preheat the oven to 180°C. Line two baking trays with baking paper.

Cut eighteen 7 cm × 6 cm rectangles from the puff pastry sheets and place on the prepared baking trays. Lightly sprinkle with caster sugar and bake for 5–6 minutes or until golden.

Place a tablespoon of chocolate mousse on top of six puff pastry rectangles, then top with another rectangle. Add another tablespoon of mousse and another rectangle to create a stack, as shown.

Dust with icing sugar, to serve.

Serves 6

Lemon Cake with Earl Grey Icing

You can't host a high tea without serving a decadent cake. Here are two of my favourite recipes (see also Rhubarb Meringue Cake on following page): both delicious show-stoppers with true 'wow' factor.

225 g (1½ cups) self-raising flour
100 g (⅔ cup) plain flour
240 g butter, softened
170 g (¾ cup) caster sugar
zest and juice of 2 lemons
3 eggs
flowers, to decorate (optional)

Earl grey icing
4 earl grey teabags
2 tablespoons boiling water
100 g butter, softened
160 g (1 cup) icing sugar, sifted

Preheat the oven to 180°C. Grease and lightly flour a 20 cm round cake tin.

Sift the flours into a bowl. In a separate large bowl, use an electric beater to cream the butter and sugar until light and fluffy. Add the lemon zest and then the eggs one at a time, mixing well after each addition. Gently fold in the flour, then add the lemon juice. Transfer the mixture to the cake tin and bake for 1 hour or until a skewer inserted into the middle comes out clean. Place on a wire rack and allow to cool before icing.

For the earl grey icing, place the teabags in a small bowl and pour over the boiling water. Set aside for 30 minutes to cool completely and allow the flavour to infuse, then squeeze each teabag to extract the liquid. Place the butter and icing sugar in a separate glass bowl and use an electric beater to beat until pale and fluffy. Slowly pour in the tea infusion and beat for 1 minute more. Use a small spatula to spread the icing over the top of the cake, creating small peaks as you work.

To serve, decorate the cake with flowers of your choice.

Serves 8

Rhubarb Meringue Cake

250 g (1⅔ cups) plain flour
45 g (¼ cup) cornflour
3 teaspoons baking powder
200 g butter, softened
440 g (2 cups) caster sugar
2 teaspoons vanilla extract
8 eggs, separated
60 ml (¼ cup) milk
1 teaspoon rose-pink
    food colouring

Rhubarb cream
4 stalks rhubarb, chopped
    into 2 cm pieces
1 vanilla bean, split and
    seeds scraped
1 tablespoon caster sugar
150 ml thickened cream

Preheat the oven to 180°C. Grease two 22 cm springform tins and line with baking paper.

Sift the flour, cornflour and baking powder into a bowl. In a separate large bowl, cream the butter and 200 g of caster sugar until light and fluffy. Add the vanilla and then the egg yolks one at a time, mixing well after each addition. Alternately fold in the flour mixture and milk. Divide the cake mixture between the two prepared tins and bake for 30 minutes or until a skewer inserted into the middle comes out clean.

Meanwhile, whisk the egg whites until soft peaks form. Gradually add the remaining sugar, continuing to beat until thick and glossy. Fold through the food colouring to create a pink swirl.

Remove the cakes from the oven and allow to cool for 10 minutes and then remove the springform sides. Line a baking tray with baking paper and place one cake on its tin base on the tray. Using a spatula, gently top one sponge with the egg white mixture and create a peaked effect. Return the cake to the oven for 10 minutes or until the egg white is starting to brown. Set aside.

For the rhubarb cream, place the rhubarb, vanilla seeds, sugar and 1 tablespoon of water in a medium saucepan. Cook for 6–8 minutes over medium heat or until the rhubarb has softened. Remove from the heat and allow to cool. Whip the cream in a bowl, then stir through the rhubarb.

Place the plain sponge on a serving platter and dollop over the rhubarb cream. Carefully balance the meringue sponge on top. Serve.

Serves 8

A
MENU BY
MATT

MATT MORAN, CO-OWNER AND
HEAD CHEF OF ARIA, IS KNOWN
FOR HIS DARING AND PANACHE.
THIS TRULY GOURMET MENU
IS PERFECT FOR A REALLY
SPECIAL OCCASION, OR RARE,
INDULGENT TREAT.

first knew Matt Moran long before his chocolate tart had become Australia's most celebrated dessert, and long before I had become a fashion designer. He is the co-owner and head chef of ARIA, a harbourside restaurant that not only boasts some of Sydney's more glorious views but some of the city's finest food. In the world of cuisine, he is known for his daring and panache: Matt Moran is like a matador of food. He also happens to be one of the nicest men in the industry.

This special, set-piece meal was prepared for a group of his friends and mine, and brought together elements from our very different worlds. Matt cooked for us in an empty photographic studio, the kind of space where we do many of our fashion shoots. And in many ways the whole evening was a study in contrasts. The clothes were as bright and colourful as the backdrop was monochromatic. The dress was formal, with the men in black tie, but the table setting was anything but, with guests perched on cushions.

Matt spent the whole day prepping, cooking and plating up, and he used the ultimate 'foodie' ingredients: caviar, truffles, scampi, pheasant. But don't be put off by the complexity of the menu, or by the exorbitant cost. For that really special occasion, it is well worth the investment of time, money and energy.

Certainly, this was one of our more memorable meals; truly a night of food, fashion and friends.

SET THE SCENE

STYLING
A LARGE WHITE SHEET FOR THE FLOOR
BLACK GAFFER TAPE TO CREATE FLOOR PLACE NAMES
A MIX OF BLACK AND WHITE CUSHIONS

FOR THE TABLE
A WHITE TABLECLOTH
VINTAGE GLASS PIECES IN ASSORTED BRIGHT COLOURS
TEALIGHTS, TO FIT INSIDE THE GLASS PIECES
BUNCHES OF WHITE FLOWERS (WE USED CYCLAMEN)
GLASS OR PERSPEX CANDELABRA AND WHITE CANDLES
MONOCHROME CROCKERY AND BLACK NAPKINS

PLAYLIST
VIVALDI *FOUR SEASONS*
FEIST *THE REMINDER*
PINK MARTINI *HANG ON LITTLE TOMATO*
JOSE PADILLA *BELLA MUSICA 4*
THE SEA AND CAKE *OUI*

ADAM

ELIZA

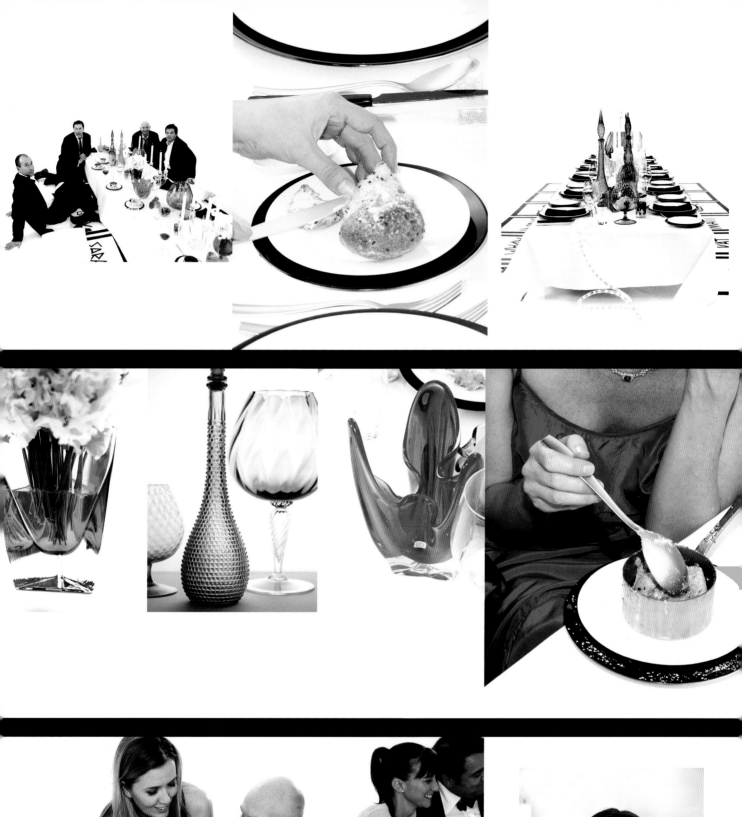

MENU

CANAPE
BLINIS WITH CAVIAR

ENTREE
BALLOTINE OF RABBIT, FOIE GRAS AND CAPOCOLLO WITH GINGERBREAD, PUMPKIN AND POMEGRANATE DRESSING

MID
SCAMPI TAILS WITH SHERRY PUREE, CAULIFLOWER AND BARLEY CRUMBS

MAIN
PHEASANT ROASTED WITH TRUFFLES

DESSERT
PRUNE AND ARMAGNAC SOUFFLE

BLINIS WITH CAVIAR

These are perfect for an intimate but indulgent dinner party.
Try and get your hands on the best caviar that you can find.

200 ml milk
8 g dried yeast
150 g (1 cup) plain flour
2 egg yolks
salt and pepper
2 egg whites
100 g sour cream
1 × 50 g tin of Sterling Royal caviar

Heat the milk in a large saucepan over medium heat. When warm, stir in the yeast until it dissolves. Remove the pan from the heat and add the flour and egg yolks. Season with salt and pepper, then beat together to form a smooth paste. Cover with a tea towel and leave in a warm place to prove for 1 hour. Stir the mixture to remove all air and leave to prove for another 10 minutes.

In a bowl, whisk the egg whites to a stiff peak and then gently fold into the batter.

Heat a non-stick frying pan over medium heat, lightly grease with a little oil and spoon in the batter to form small pancakes 3 cm wide. Leave to cook for 1 minute before turning over and cooking for 1 more minute on the other side. Remove the blinis from the pan and leave to cool on a wire rack. Repeat the process until all the batter has been used.

To serve, place a teaspoon of sour cream onto each blini and top with caviar.

Serves 6

A MENU BY MATT

BALLOTINE OF RABBIT, FOIE GRAS AND CAPOCOLLO WITH GINGERBREAD, PUMPKIN AND POMEGRANATE DRESSING

A perfect entree to serve in autumn, this dish takes some time but it is worth the effort. Rabbit needs to be cooked carefully as it has a low fat percentage and can easily dry out.

200 g butternut pumpkin, peeled and cut
    into 2 cm dice
tiny frisee leaves, to garnish

Chicken liver parfait
butter, for pan-frying
1 golden shallot, sliced
1 clove garlic, sliced
1 bay leaf
1 sprig thyme
100 ml brandy
100 ml port
100 ml madeira
600 g chicken liver, sinew discarded
190 g butter, at room temperature
3 eggs, at room temperature
1 egg yolk, at room temperature
1 teaspoon each salt and pepper

Rabbit ballotine
1 kg duck fat
50 ml white wine
1 bouquet garni
1 carrot, peeled
4 cloves garlic, peeled
4 white rabbit shoulders
40 g pistachios, roasted and chopped
4 white rabbit loins
salt and pepper
15 slices capocollo or prosciutto,
    thinly sliced
100 g foie gras, sliced into batons

For the chicken liver parfait, heat a little butter in a small saucepan over low heat, then add the shallot, garlic, bay leaf and thyme, and fry for 2 minutes. Add the brandy, port and madeira, and cook until the liquid has reduced by half. Remove the pan from the heat and strain the liquid into a glass or ceramic bowl, discarding the shallot, garlic and herbs. Set the liquid aside to cool. Add the chicken livers to the bowl, then cover and marinate for 24 hours in the fridge.

The next day, preheat the oven to 120°C. Remove the marinated chicken livers from the fridge and add the butter, eggs and egg yolk. Mix well and season with salt and pepper. Transfer the mixture to a blender and puree until smooth. Taste for seasoning. Pass the mixture through a fine sieve, then spoon into a small terrine mould. Cover with baking paper, secure with a lid of foil and place into a roasting tin. Fill the tin with enough water to come halfway up the sides of the mould. Bake for 40 minutes or until the parfait is set. Cool, then store in the fridge. (Leftovers can be kept in the fridge overnight, then eaten with toast for supper the next day.)

Next, make the filling for the rabbit ballotine. Heat the duck fat, wine, bouquet garni, carrot, garlic and 50 ml of water in a large, lidded ovenproof saucepan or flameproof casserole dish over low heat. Add the rabbit shoulders and bring to a simmer. Cover with buttered baking paper and the lid. Cook slowly in the oven for 2½ hours at 120°C or until the shoulders are tender. Remove from the oven and leave the shoulders to cool in the fat. Once cool, remove the meat and vegetables from the fat and keep the fat to one side. Separate the rabbit meat from the bones and shred the meat. Transfer to a large bowl. Grate the carrot and mash the garlic, then add to the shredded meat along with the pistachios and 200 g of the fat. Place the rabbit meat mixture over a bowl of ice and mix together until cold – this will lower the temperature quickly to assist in setting the fat. Keep the ballotine filling at room temperature.

Season the rabbit loins with salt and pepper. Wrap tightly in plastic film, then place in a large saucepan and cover with simmering water. Simmer for 10 minutes, then leave to rest for 10 minutes before unwrapping. Using a sharp knife, thinly slice the rabbit loins lengthways. Lay a piece of plastic film measuring approximately 60 cm × 45 cm on the work surface. Starting on one short side of the film, alternate layers of the sliced rabbit loin and the capocollo slices, making sure they overlap. Continue this until all the rabbit and capocollo slices have been used and most of the plastic film is covered.

Gingerbread
60 g butter
60 g brown sugar
80 g molasses
35 g pomegranate molasses
1 egg, at room temperature
115 g plain flour
1 teaspoon ground ginger
½ teaspoon allspice powder
½ teaspoon baking powder
½ teaspoon bicarbonate of soda
½ teaspoon salt

Pomegranate dressing
200 ml pomegranate juice
50 g caster sugar
50 g pomegranate molasses
1–2 pomegranates, seeds removed

Place the ballotine filling down the centre, making a gully as you go. Place the foie gras batons in the gully. Place more filling over the foie gras and then tightly wrap in the sliced rabbit and capocollo to make a roll. Tie each end of the plastic film with string and place in the fridge to set. When cold, slice with a sharp knife into 12 slices then remove the plastic film. Store in the fridge until required.

Increase the oven temperature to 160°C.

For the gingerbread, use an electric mixer to combine the butter and brown sugar until light and fluffy. Add the molasses, pomegranate molasses and egg, and continue to mix until thoroughly combined. Sieve the plain flour, ginger, allspice, baking powder, bicarbonate of soda and salt together in a bowl then fold into the butter and sugar mixture. Mix until smooth. Line a cake tin with baking paper and pour in the gingerbread batter. Bake for 30 minutes or until golden brown, then cool on a wire rack. Once cool, set aside half of the gingerbread then place the remaining gingerbread in a food processor. Using the pulse setting, blend the gingerbread into crumbs. Set aside.

For the pomegranate dressing, place the pomegranate juice and sugar in a small saucepan, and cook until reduced by half. Stir in the pomegranate molasses and seeds (reserving some seeds for serving). Remove from the heat, and store in the fridge until required. (Leftover dressing can be stored in the fridge for up to four days – try serving it with any leftover parfait.)

For the gingerbread puree, place the reserved gingerbread in a blender with 50 ml of water, and blend to make a paste. Pass through a fine sieve to ensure it is smooth.

Cook the pumpkin in boiling water for 2 minutes or until tender, then drain.

To serve, smear a teaspoon of the gingerbread puree on each plate and place 2 overlapping slices of rabbit ballotine next to it. Make a quenelle of the chicken liver parfait using two hot teaspoons or simply place a spoonful alongside the ballotine. Sprinkle gingerbread crumbs over the parfait. Arrange cubes of pumpkin in a circle around the plate. To finish, dot around the pomegranate dressing, scatter a few pomegranate seeds on the plate and garnish with frisee leaves.

Serves 6

SOMETIMES
A RECIPE IS
SO VERY EXQUISITE,
SO VERY DELICIOUS,
THAT YOU
JUST HAVE TO
COOK IT
FOR FRIENDS.

SCAMPI TAILS WITH SHERRY PUREE, CAULIFLOWER AND BARLEY CRUMBS

Incredibly sweet and succulent, the scampi tails combine perfectly with
the sweetness of the sherry puree and the nuttiness of the roasted barley.

vegetable oil, for frying
12 scampi tails, peeled
knob of butter
chervil, to garnish

Sherry puree
75 g caster sugar
350 ml Ollo Rosso (sweet) sherry
1 teaspoon Texturas Gellan
    (available from speciality
    food shops)

Cauliflower puree
250 g cauliflower, finely chopped
20 g unsalted butter
pinch of salt
125 ml (½ cup) milk
50 ml cream

Barley crumbs
1 tablespoon pearl barley
1 teaspoon vegetable oil
1 tablespoon slivered almonds
1 slice prosciutto
3 teaspoons chopped chives

Cauliflower tempura
100 g (⅔ cup) flour
50 g cornflour
50 g baking powder
1 teaspoon salt
250 g cauliflower florets,
    blanched

For the sherry puree, make a sugar syrup by combining 75 ml of water and the caster sugar in a small saucepan, and cook over medium heat until the mixture is reduced by half. Place the sherry in a separate saucepan and cook over medium heat until reduced by half. Add the sugar syrup to the sherry, then whisk in the Texturas Gellan and boil for 1 minute. Strain the mixture into a bowl and leave to set in the fridge. Cut the sherry gel into chunks then blend to a smooth puree in a blender or small food processor, and set aside. (The sherry will go cloudy.) Any leftover sherry puree can be stored in the fridge for up to three months.

For the cauliflower puree, gently cook the cauliflower in the butter with a little salt for 5 minutes. Pour in the milk and cover with a lid. Cook the cauliflower over high heat until the milk has evaporated. Place the cauliflower in a blender and add the cream. Blend until smooth, then transfer to a bowl and set aside.

Preheat the oven to 180°C.

For the barley crumbs, place the barley in a small saucepan, cover with water and simmer for 20 minutes or until tender, then drain. Heat the vegetable oil in a separate saucepan. Add the cooked pearl barley and fry for 3–4 minutes or until golden brown, then remove from the heat and drain on paper towel. Place the slivered almonds on a baking tray and toast in the oven for 4–5 minutes, watching carefully as they burn easily. Mix the barley with the toasted almonds. Very finely chop the mixture with the prosciutto, then place the crumbs in a bowl and mix in the chopped chives. Set aside.

For the cauliflower tempura batter, mix together the flour, cornflour, baking powder, 250 ml (1 cup) of water and salt until combined. Pour vegetable oil into a deep fryer or large heavy-based saucepan until two-thirds full and heat to 180°C. (To check the temperature without a thermometer, drop a cube of bread into the oil. The bread will brown in about 15 seconds if the oil is hot enough.) Dip the blanched cauliflower florets into the batter, shaking off any excess. Deep-fry for 2 minutes or until crispy. Season with a little salt and set aside.

Heat a little oil in a frying pan and, when hot, add the scampi tails. Add a knob of butter to the pan and sauté the scampi for 1 minute before turning over and cooking for another minute.

To serve, gently reheat the cauliflower puree. Place a spoonful of the sherry puree in the centre of each plate then arrange 2 scampi tails and some cauliflower tempura around it. Spoon some cauliflower puree on top of the sherry puree and sprinkle over the barley crumbs. Garnish with chervil sprigs and serve immediately.

Serves 6

PHEASANT ROASTED WITH TRUFFLES

Australian truffles make the perfect accompaniment to the pheasant —
the black jewels from Western Australia are exquisite.

20 g fresh truffle
3 pheasants, legs and
   wishbones removed
3 sprigs thyme
3 cloves garlic, crushed
150 g butter
1 tablespoon brandy
1 tablespoon port
1 tablespoon madeira

1 litre veal stock
7 parsnips
salt and pepper
vegetable oil, for deep-frying,
   plus 2 tablespoons extra
chervil sprigs, to garnish

Slice 12 thin slices of truffle using a truffle slicer. Work your fingers under the skin of the pheasant breasts to loosen them and place 2 slices of truffle under the skin of each breast. Place 1 sprig of thyme and 1 crushed garlic clove inside the cavity of each pheasant, and place in the fridge until ready to roast.

For the truffle sauce, finely chop half of the remaining truffle. Place a tablespoon of butter in a medium saucepan and add the chopped truffle. Gently cook over low heat for 10 minutes then add the brandy, port and madeira, and gently simmer until the liquid has reduced by half. Add the stock, bring to the boil then turn down to a simmer and cook until reduced by half. Set the truffle sauce aside until required.

For the parsnip puree, peel and finely slice 3 of the parsnips. Heat a tablespoon of butter in a heavy-based saucepan over medium heat and add the sliced parsnips. Season with a little salt and pepper, then add 100 ml of water and cover with a lid. Cook slowly for 10–15 minutes, stirring occasionally, until the parsnips have broken down. Transfer the mixture to a blender and puree until smooth and silky. Set aside.

For the parsnip chips, pour the vegetable oil into a deep fryer or large heavy-based saucepan until two-thirds full and heat to 160°C. (To check the temperature without a thermometer, drop a cube of bread into the oil. The bread will brown in about 30 seconds if the oil is hot enough.) Peel 1 parsnip and cut into strips using a vegetable peeler. Deep-fry the parsnip strips in the oil until golden brown, then drain on paper towel. Season lightly with a little salt and set aside.

Preheat the oven to 180°C.

Peel the remaining 3 parsnips and cut into batons. Place in a saucepan and cover with cold water and a good pinch of salt. Bring to the boil and simmer for 2 minutes before draining. Place the parsnips in iced water to refresh, then drain again. Set aside until required.

Heat a tablespoon of oil in a large ovenproof frying pan over high heat. Season the pheasants with salt and pepper. Place them, breast-side down, in the frying pan and fry gently for 1 minute or until lightly golden. Turn the pheasants over and fry gently for another minute. Transfer the frying pan to the oven and cook for a further 5 minutes. Turn the pheasants over again and cook for 5 minutes. Turn the pheasants onto their backs and cook for 5 minutes. Remove the pheasants from the oven and leave to rest in a warm place for 10 minutes.

Heat a tablespoon of oil and the remaining butter in a separate frying pan until foaming. Add the parsnip batons and saute for 3–4 minutes until golden brown.

To serve, gently reheat the truffle sauce and the parsnip puree. Remove the breasts of each pheasant and carve each breast into four. Smear some of the parsnip puree onto each serving plate and add a carved pheasant breast. Place a pile of the parsnip batons next to it and place a few parsnip chips on top. Spoon the truffle sauce over and around the breast and finely shave the remaining truffle over the plate. Garnish with chervil and serve immediately.

Serves 6

PRUNE AND ARMAGNAC SOUFFLE

When you are making souffles, the most important thing is to make sure that all the equipment — the whisk, bowls and souffle dish — is spotlessly clean and devoid of any fat or water. This will ensure that your souffles rise to the occasion every time.

125 g caster sugar, plus extra to dust
80 ml armagnac
80 g cornflour
250 g prunes
unsalted butter, for greasing
10 egg whites
300 ml cream, whipped

Place 200 ml of water, 25 g of sugar and the armagnac in a medium-sized saucepan and bring to the boil. In a bowl, mix the cornflour with 50 ml of water, then whisk into the hot syrup. Add the prunes to the pan and bring back to the boil, then simmer for 2 minutes. Place the mixture in a blender and puree to a smooth paste. Transfer the prune puree to a large bowl and set aside.

Preheat the oven to 160°C. Lightly grease six copper pots or ramekins with unsalted butter and dust with sugar. Place in the fridge until required.

In a bowl, whisk the egg whites to a soft peak. Add the remaining 100 g of sugar and continue to whisk until shiny and stiff. Using a spatula, gently fold the egg whites into the prune puree.

Spoon the souffle mixture into the prepared pots and smooth the tops with a pallet knife. Bake for 6 minutes or until well risen.

Serve immediately with the whipped cream on the side.

Serves 6

A MENU BY MATT

BONNIE'S BIRTHDAY

BUBBLES, KALEIDOSCOPE JELLY CAKE, CHOCOLATE AND STRAWBERRY STARS. ALICE IN WONDERLAND MEETS BANKSY. KID HEAVEN.

Bonnie is the daughter of my best friend from school, Schaan, and one of my godchildren. She is as smart as she is cute, and has a ludicrously wide vocabulary that belies her tender age. So to celebrate her birthday, we laid on a pretend grown-up dinner party.

We used my very best china, borrowed my mum's silver cutlery, silver teapots and silver trays, and used fragile vintage glass. People thought we were crazy – for a time, I did, too – but we explained to the kids that the china was extremely precious and, in the end, all of it escaped unscathed and unchipped. We also ran up some chair covers, with black-and-white bows. Very quick and very simple.

To dress the kids, I raided my vintage collection and came up with the ultimate dress-up box. Couture for kids, I guess you could call it. Then we got a graffiti artist to come in to spray-paint the backdrop – kind of *Alice in Wonderland* meets Banksy. For jewellery, we let the kids make it themselves (out of ribbons and lollies). For flowers, we got big bunches of daisies that cost hardly anything. And we cheated with the birthday cake – rather than slaving for hours to create a work of art that would be demolished in seconds, we bought an amazing cake from Princess Cupcake in Sydney.

Although the kids were little angels on the day, I have to admit that this is a less than saintly menu. As I talked through the devilishly sweet recipes with Bonnie's mum, she nervously asked if I was 'at least serving some fruit'. So I've smuggled in some berry goodness among the ice-cream, chocolate and rice bubble crackle. You may decide to include some healthier, low-sugar options on the day. But I know that when I was a kid, I loved every single one of these treats – and birthdays come but once a year, after all . . .

SET THE SCENE

STYLING

A large white sheet for the backdrop
White lampshades and old white furniture
Cans of spray-paint in bright colours
Child-sized chairs, covered with black fabric
Black-and-white striped fabric (to create bows for chairs)
A birdcage and white ceramic bunnies
A bubble machine and a trampoline
Assortment of dress-up clothes, hats and jewellery
Mixed lollies and ribbon (to make the sweet jewellery
    and for party games)

FOR THE TABLE

A white sheet, spray-painted
Silver platters and goblets
Vintage glassware and cake stands
Handfuls of glitter and silver stars
Brightly coloured vases filled with daisies
Even more mixed lollies

PLAYLIST

The Beatles *Yellow Submarine*
Yo Gabba Gabba! *Music is . . . Awesome!*
They Might Be Giants *Here Come the ABC's*
Sesame Street *Hot! Hot! Hot! Dance Songs*
Various Artists *Motown: The Classic Years*

MENU

***

BERRY MILK

MARSHMALLOW BISCUITS

TOASTED CHOCOLATE AND STRAWBERRY STARS

ANIMAL PUFFS

BAKED BEAN VOL-AU-VENTS

BLUEBERRY RIPPLE ICE-CREAM SUNDAE

KALEIDOSCOPE JELLY CAKE

BERRY MILK

Forget about fizzy drinks laden with artificial everything and whiz up this fruit smoothie instead.

225 g (1½ cups) frozen raspberries
    or blueberries
750 ml (3 cups) milk
750 ml vanilla ice-cream
honey, to taste

Combine all of the ingredients in a blender and blend until smooth.

Pour into chilled glasses or a jug, and serve immediately.

Serves 6

MARSHMALLOW BISCUITS

These are great fun to make. Assorted sprinkles are available from speciality cake-decorating shops – try hundreds and thousands, edible glitter and silver cachous.

150 g marshmallows
1 tablespoon boiling water
15 milk arrowroot or other sweet biscuits
assorted sprinkles, to decorate

Place the marshmallows and boiling water in a heatproof bowl over a saucepan of gently simmering water (making sure the bottom of the bowl does not touch). Heat, stirring occasionally, for 10–15 minutes or until melted.

Using a metal spatula, spread the melted marshmallow over the top of the biscuits. Decorate with sprinkles, to serve.

Makes 15

TOASTED CHOCOLATE AND STRAWBERRY STARS

For a grown-up version of these toasted chocolate sandwiches, replace the sliced white bread with freshly baked sourdough.

12 slices white bread
salted butter, softened, for buttering bread
50 g good-quality dark chocolate (70% cocoa),
    finely chopped
6 small strawberries, hulled and thinly
    sliced lengthways, plus extra to
    garnish (optional)
icing sugar, for dusting

Using a 9 cm star-shaped cutter, cut a star from each slice of bread.

Spread both sides of each star with a little butter. Evenly scatter the chocolate over half of the slices, then arrange the strawberry slices on top. Top with the remaining bread slices, pressing gently to stick.

Heat a non-stick frying pan over medium heat and fry the sandwiches for 1 minute on each side or until golden.

Dust with icing sugar and serve immediately, garnished with extra strawberries, if desired.

Serves 6

ANIMAL PUFFS

Kids love helping to make these puff-pastry bites. If you don't have animal-shaped cutters, try stars and moons instead.

3 sheets ready-rolled puff pastry
1 egg, lightly beaten

Creamed corn filling
20 g butter
1 small brown onion, finely chopped
50 g pancetta or bacon, finely chopped
2 corn cobs, kernels removed
60 ml (¼ cup) chicken stock
1 tablespoon finely chopped parsley
sea salt and freshly ground black pepper

For the creamed corn filling, melt the butter in a medium saucepan over medium heat, then add the onion and pancetta. Cook, stirring, for 5–7 minutes or until soft. Stir in the corn kernels and add the chicken stock. Bring to the boil, then reduce the heat to low and simmer for 10–15 minutes, until the liquid has almost evaporated and the corn is tender. Add the parsley and season to taste with salt and pepper.

Using a stick blender or food processor, blend the corn mixture until smooth, then allow to cool. (The creamed corn can be stored in an airtight container in the fridge for up to three days.)

Preheat the oven to 180°C and line a baking tray with baking paper. Using animal-shaped cutters, cut the puff pastry sheets into pairs of shapes. Spoon a little of the creamed corn filling onto half of the shapes, leaving a 5 mm border. Brush the edges with egg. Top with the corresponding shape and use a fork or your fingers to seal the edges. Place on the prepared tray and brush with egg.

Bake the animal puffs for 15–20 minutes or until crisp and golden.

Serves 6

BAKED BEAN VOL-AU-VENTS

When I was growing up, vol-au-vents seemed the height of sophistication. The kids at Bonnie's birthday were similarly impressed. Look for the cases in speciality food stores or in the bakery section of supermarkets.

24 vol-au-vent cases
1 egg, lightly beaten

Baked beans
1 small brown onion, coarsely chopped
1 small carrot, coarsely chopped
1 clove garlic, crushed
1 tablespoon olive oil
sea salt and freshly ground black pepper
1 × 400 g can cannellini beans, drained and rinsed
200 g chopped tomatoes
2 teaspoons finely chopped parsley

For the baked beans, blend the onion, carrot and garlic in a food processor until finely chopped. Heat the olive oil in a frying pan over medium heat. Cook the chopped onion, carrot and garlic for 5–7 minutes or until softened. Season to taste with salt and pepper.

Add the cannellini beans, tomato and 60 ml (¼ cup) of water, and bring just to the boil. Reduce the heat to low and simmer gently, stirring occasionally, for 10–15 minutes or until the sauce is thick. Remove from the heat and stir through the parsley.

Preheat the oven to 180°C and line a baking tray with baking paper. Spoon a teaspoon of baked beans into each vol-au-vent and place on the prepared tray. (Store leftover beans in an airtight container in the fridge for up to one week.) Brush the vol-au-vents with egg. Bake for 5–10 minutes or until heated through.

Serve immediately.

Serves 6

BLUEBERRY RIPPLE ICE-CREAM SUNDAE

For this recipe you'll need to prepare the ice-cream the day before. Make the rice bubble crackle in advance too (keep in an airtight container between layers of baking paper) and on the day you can simply scoop, sprinkle and serve.

2 litres vanilla ice-cream
1 × 125 g punnet blueberries
hundreds and thousands, to decorate

Rice bubble crackle
220 g (1 cup) caster sugar
15 g (½ cup) rice bubbles

Stand the ice-cream at room temperature for 10–15 minutes until softened.

Place the blueberries and 1 tablespoon of water in a small saucepan over low heat. Cook for 5–10 minutes or until the blueberries have softened and the liquid is starting to thicken.

Spoon the ice-cream into a large bowl, reserving the container, and stir through the blueberries. Gently fold until just combined, being careful not to over-stir. Return the ice-cream to its container and freeze overnight until firm.

For the rice bubble crackle, combine the caster sugar and 125 ml (½ cup) of water in a saucepan over medium heat, stirring until the sugar dissolves. Increase the heat to medium–high and simmer, without stirring, for 5–7 minutes or until caramel in colour.

Meanwhile, lay a sheet of baking paper on a flat work surface and sprinkle with rice bubbles. Pour the caramel evenly over the top. Cool completely, and then break into pieces.

To serve, spoon out the ice-cream and scatter with hundreds and thousands. Serve with a piece of rice bubble crackle.

Serves 6–8

KALEIDOSCOPE JELLY CAKE

My friend Kristina made this for her daughter's birthday. It was such a hit, I had to include it in the book. You'll need to refrigerate the jelly overnight to allow it to set.

5 × 85 g packets jelly crystals (5 different flavours)
2½ tablespoons powdered gelatine

Rinse a 25 cm × 20 cm plastic container (2.5 litre capacity) with water, then line with plastic film.

Combine one packet of jelly crystals with 2 teaspoons of gelatine in a large heatproof jug, and follow the jelly packet instructions. Pour the mixture into the prepared container. Chill in the freezer for 15–20 minutes until almost set.

Meanwhile, as the first jelly layer sets, prepare another packet of jelly crystals and allow to cool at room temperature, stirring occasionally.

Remove the first jelly from the freezer, then gently pour the cooled jelly mixture over the back of a spoon onto the set jelly. Return to the freezer and chill for 15–20 minutes until almost set.

Repeat three more times with the remaining jelly crystals and gelatine powder. Refrigerate the jelly overnight.

The next day, turn out the jelly onto a chopping board lined with plastic film. Use a wet knife to cut the jelly into thick slices and serve.

Serves 6–8

Cloud 9

CELEBRATE A MATCH MADE IN
HEAVEN WITH ANGEL WINGS,
CERAMIC SWANS AND A GENEROUS,
HEART-WARMING DINNER.

rad Ngata has been doing my hair since I was nineteen. I was a shop assistant at the time at a store on Oxford Street in Sydney, when a friend came rushing in to tell me about an amazing stylist down the road that I had to go visit. Thankfully, I took her advice, and it was love at first sight. Brad and his boyfriend Glenn Chaplin have been my 'besties' pretty much ever since.

Brad does the hair direction for all of my fashion shows and all of my photo-shoots. He also looked after me on my wedding day in Sri Lanka, what could have been a really bad hair day with 100-degree heat and almost 100 per cent humidity. Suffice to say, he performed heroics.

Brad and Glenn have been together for fifteen years, so to celebrate that anniversary we put on a dinner for them and their closest friends.

I wanted the evening to be as heavenly as possible, so we tried to make the space look like a little slice of heaven. We started with the clouds and the stars – it's amazing what you can pull off with the help of a Xerox machine – and found the angel wings for the chair-backs at a $2 shop. Over the years, I've amassed a big collection of ceramic swans, so they became the centrepiece for the table. The swans also became the motif for the whole evening, which seemed especially fitting – they not only mate for life, but have gay relationships.

The boys love homey, fifties-style dishes, so we came up with a menu that offered warming comfort food on a cold winter night. And you'll be glad to hear that the swan theme did not extend to the kitchen: we were not working furiously behind-the-scenes while everything was beautiful and graceful on the surface. I wanted to spend the night celebrating rather than cooking, so this is not a tricky menu. The macaroni can be prepared in advance and the roast pork is deceptively simple for a dish that looks so impressive. As for dessert, Glenn insisted on having pavlova so I introduced him to Eton mess, the English answer to the classic Aussie dish. It's one of my favourites and oh-so-easy (even easier if you buy the meringue instead of making your own). Glenn is a convert, and I'm sure you will be too.

SET THE SCENE

STYLING

A4 photocopies of stars and clouds,
  stuck to the wall (or a black sheet,
  if you prefer)
Sackfuls of cotton wool, to create clouds
Angel wings, pink silk and taffeta,
  to cover chairs

FOR THE TABLE

A black tablecloth
Vintage ceramic swan vases filled
  with pink and white carnations
Gold candles
Mix-and-match gold cutlery and
  gold-trimmed china

PLAYLIST

Various Artists *Jazz & 80's*
Pet Shop Boys *Pop Art: The Hits*
Blondie *Parallel Lines*
Madonna *Any album*
Dimitri from Paris *Cocktail Disco*

TO START
Kir royale
Salmon mousse with croutons

.

ENTREE
Herbed pecorino macaroni

.

MAIN
Roast pork rack with whole baked apples
Brussels sprout salad with pancetta
Roasted pumpkin wedges

.

DESSERT
Raspberry Eton mess

.

PETIT FOUR
Minted dark chocolate truffles

.

KIR ROYALE

This classic aperitif is making its way back onto cocktail
party menus. It's a very simple way to do something different.

750 ml champagne
180 ml creme de cassis

Divide the creme de cassis between six glasses and
top with champagne to create a 'blushed' colour.

Serves 6

SALMON MOUSSE WITH CROUTONS

An elegant dish that looks and tastes divine – and it's really easy to prepare.
You can, of course, use any shaped tin. Hot-smoked salmon portions are
available from good delis and larger supermarkets.

500 g (2 cups) creme fraiche
1 large handful parsley leaves, finely chopped
1 large handful dill, finely chopped
1 large handful mint leaves, finely chopped
500 g hot-smoked salmon portions, skin and bloodline removed
2 tablespoons capers
1 tablespoon finely grated lemon zest
2 teaspoons lemon juice
sea salt and cracked black pepper
1 thin sourdough baguette

Whisk the creme fraiche for 1 minute or until stiff peaks form. Chill in the fridge for 15 minutes.

Meanwhile, lightly grease a 750 ml (3 cup) capacity heart-shaped tin and line with plastic film.
(Allow plenty of excess to overhang on each of the long sides to wrap around the mousse
later.) Combine the herbs in a small bowl and sprinkle evenly over the base of the tin.

Blend the salmon in a food processor for 30 seconds or until a paste forms. Combine the
salmon, capers, lemon zest and juice in a bowl and season with salt and pepper. Fold through
the creme fraiche and then spoon the mixture into the tin. Wrap the mousse in the overhanging
plastic film and refrigerate for 3–4 hours or until set.

To make the croutons, preheat the oven to 150°C. Thinly slice the baguette into 5 mm pieces
and lay in a single layer on a baking tray. Cook for 1–2 minutes on each side or until dry and crisp.

Unwrap the mousse and use the plastic film to turn it out onto a platter. Serve with croutons.

Serves 6–8

CLOUD 9

HERBED PECORINO MACARONI

You can make this the night before. Cover the filled dishes with plastic film and place them in the fridge. Bring out two hours before guests arrive to allow the macaroni to come up to room temperature. Crumble over the goat's cheese and bake just before serving. Easy.

300 g macaroni
625 ml (2½ cups) milk
1 bay leaf
2 sprigs thyme
3 peppercorns
2 tablespoons butter
2 tablespoons plain flour
40 g (½ cup) grated pecorino
40 g (½ cup) grated parmesan
1 tablespoon chopped chervil, plus extra to garnish
pinch of freshly grated nutmeg
20 g goat's cheese

Cook the macaroni in a large saucepan of boiling, salted water until al dente.

Combine the milk, bay leaf, thyme and peppercorns in a small saucepan and bring just to the boil. Turn off the heat and allow the mixture to infuse for 30 minutes. Discard the herbs.

Preheat the oven to 180°C. Melt the butter in a medium saucepan, sprinkle over the flour and cook, stirring continuously, for 1–2 minutes or until the flour starts to brown. Slowly whisk in the infused milk until well combined. Continue to stir for 4–6 minutes or until the sauce thickens. Stir in the macaroni, pecorino, parmesan, chervil and nutmeg.

Spoon the macaroni into six 250 ml (1 cup) capacity dishes and crumble over the goat's cheese. Bake for 10 minutes or until the cheese melts and turns golden. Serve garnished with chervil.

Serves 6

CLOUD 9

ROAST PORK RACK WITH WHOLE BAKED APPLES

Comfort food with class. You can't go wrong with the mouth-watering combination of crispy, succulent pork and juicy apples. Most of us have bad memories of the brussels sprouts we were force-fed in childhood – the secret to making them delicious is adding lots of butter and something salty. We used pancetta here, but chilli or anchovies also do the trick.

1 tablespoon fennel seeds
1 tablespoon sea salt
1 tablespoon olive oil
2 kg pork rack (8 bones), scored
2 red onions, peeled and cut into wedges
1 bulb of garlic, cut in half across the middle
30 g butter, melted
1 teaspoon ground cinnamon
3 granny smith apples
3 pink lady apples
200 ml white wine
120 ml veal stock

Preheat the oven to 220°C. Grind the fennel and salt in a mortar and pestle. Rub the oil into the pork skin and then the salt mixture. Place the onion and garlic in a large roasting tin and sit the pork on top. Roast for 20–25 minutes or until the skin is brown and crisp. Reduce the heat to 180°C and cook for a further 20 minutes.

Combine the butter and cinnamon in a small bowl. Use a small sharp knife to score the apples around the centre – this will stop them exploding. Place them around the pork in the roasting tin. Pour the butter mixture over the apples and cook for 20–25 minutes or until the apples are soft and the juices from the pork run clear when the meat is pierced with a skewer. Remove the apples and pork from the tin and cover with foil to keep warm.

Place the roasting tin over two burners and scrape with a wooden spoon to release the good bits stuck to the bottom. Pour in the white wine and boil for 1–2 minutes or until the sauce has thickened. Strain the liquid into a saucepan, add the stock and bring to the boil. Reduce the heat and simmer for 15–20 minutes while you carve the pork.

Serve the pork with the cinnamon-butter apples, brussels sprout salad and pumpkin wedges (see recipes opposite), with the white-wine sauce poured over the top.

Serves 6

BRUSSELS SPROUT SALAD WITH PANCETTA

150 g pancetta, diced
50 g butter
2 cloves garlic, thinly sliced
400 g (about 24) brussels sprouts, hard inner core discarded

Heat a large frying pan over medium heat and cook the pancetta for 3–4 minutes or until brown and crisp. Add the butter and garlic, and cook for a further 2 minutes.

Add the brussels sprout leaves and toss to coat with the butter. Cook for 3–4 minutes or until the leaves have wilted.

Serves 6

ROASTED PUMPKIN WEDGES

2 kg baby blue pumpkin, cut into 4 cm wedges
2 tablespoons olive oil
sea salt and cracked black pepper

Preheat the oven to 180°C. In a large bowl, toss the pumpkin with olive oil, and season with salt and pepper.

Place the pumpkin on a baking tray and roast for 30 minutes. Turn and roast for another 20 minutes or until soft and caramelised.

Serves 6

RASPBERRY ETON MESS

For less fuss on the day, make the meringue the day before and store it overnight in an airtight container. Assemble the dessert just before serving so that the meringue remains crisp.

500 g raspberries
1 vanilla bean, split and seeds scraped
1 tablespoon lemon juice
110 g (½ cup) caster sugar
300 ml thickened cream

Meringue
2 egg whites
110 g (½ cup) caster sugar
¼ teaspoon vanilla extract

Preheat the oven to 150°C. Line a baking tray with baking paper.

For the meringue, beat the egg whites in a medium bowl until stiff peaks form. Slowly pour in the sugar, beating continuously, until the mixture is glossy and firm, then beat in the vanilla extract. Place tablespoons of the meringue mixture onto the prepared tray and bake for 1 hour or until crisp.

Turn off the oven, open the door slightly and allow the meringues to cool for 3–4 hours.

Place half of the raspberries and the vanilla seeds, lemon juice and sugar in a food processor and process until smooth. Refrigerate until required.

Using a balloon whisk, whisk the cream in a large glass bowl until firm peaks form. Crumble the meringue onto the cream and fold through with the processed raspberries and whole raspberries (reserving some to garnish).

To serve, spoon into dessert glasses and garnish with raspberries.

Serves 6

MINTED DARK CHOCOLATE TRUFFLES

Truffles sound tricky to make but really it's all about getting the ratio of chocolate to cream correct. Then all you need to do is choose your favourite centre or coating. We went for a fresh mint sugar: perfect after such a rich, indulgent meal.

1 bunch mint
110 g (½ cup) caster sugar, plus 1 tablespoon extra
250 ml (1 cup) cream
500 g dark chocolate, broken into small pieces
1 egg white, lightly whisked

Dry the mint well with paper towel. Place the mint (reserving about 8–10 leaves to garnish) and the sugar into a food processor and blend for 4–5 minutes or until the mixture resembles fine green sugar. Leave uncovered to dry.

Heat the cream in a large saucepan and bring just to the boil. Remove from the heat and stir in the chocolate. Continue to stir until the mixture is thick and well combined. (If the chocolate has not completely melted, return the pan to the stove over a gentle heat and stir to combine.) Transfer the mixture to a bowl and chill in the fridge for 2 hours.

Line two trays with baking paper. Dip the reserved mint leaves into the egg white, then transfer to one of the trays and dust with the extra sugar. Leave to set for 20 minutes.

Remove the chocolate mixture from the fridge and, working quickly, take out 1 tablespoon at a time and use the palm of your hand to form a ball. Place on the other prepared tray. Dust the truffles with the mint sugar and roll until well coated. Allow to set for 10 minutes, then serve on a plate, garnished with the sugared mint leaves.

Makes 24

Friends should the food, never I always clear morning after.

share
the dishes.
up the

Summer Storm

This nostalgic summer-holiday menu is perfect for down-time with friends at work or play.

food and fashion always come together at lunchtime on a shoot day. There's an unwritten rule in the industry that the designer lays on a spread. But as a novice, back when I first started out, nobody had ever thought to tell me. So when lunchtime rolled around on my first-ever shoot, I was looking to nip out for quick sandwich while everyone else was looking for a table laden with gastronomic delights. I had committed a terrible food-fashion faux pas.

Ten years on, I've not made the same mistake again, and have come to appreciate that lunch with the team – the photographer, stylist, assistants, hair and make-up, and models – is one of the most important parts of the day. To make the shoots look so effortlessly beautiful, you normally have to work hard from dawn until dusk, so lunch is just about the only time to stop, have a rest and enjoy some down-time together. And often, this mix of food and fashion can end up producing lasting friendships.

For this particular shoot, featuring the outfits in our summer collection, we travelled to Hyams Beach, a small seaside town a couple of hours south of Sydney. Hyams has always been a favourite beach of mine, mainly for the incredible pure white sand – the whitest in the world, according to the record books. It seemed the ideal location, but the problem was that the weather was far from perfect. When we set out at 5 a.m. from Sydney for the car ride down, the forecast was for heavy storms and gale-force winds – just about the last thing you need when shooting a summer collection on a beach. But the foreboding skies in the distance, with sunlight occasionally breaking through the clouds, ended up giving us the most fabulous of backdrops. They also provided the name for the collection – what else, but 'Summer Storm'.

The shoot at the beach reminded me of trips to the coast as a child, and I wanted to recreate that kind of nostalgic feel with the food. So the food theme for the day developed by Daniel Johnston became 'Aussie milk bar gone posh'. Lunch was burgers, but with soft-shell crab. Chips were also on the menu, but torn, Italian-style and flavoured with herbs.

Afternoon tea is another important break in the day, partly because it comes at the very moment when energy levels start to drop, and partly because it comes just before that time loved by photographers when the fading light is at its most perfect. Sugar-hits don't come much better than rich vanilla slices or lamingtons filled with cream and berries, especially when served with piping-hot chai.

As you'll notice, there's nothing particularly fancy about how the food is presented – it's stacked up on chopping boards and served in paper. This is a great menu to make for friends over the summer holidays.

If you are wondering about that beautiful antique bed, it has special sentimental value. It's actually an Indian wedding pavilion, which is particularly fitting because I met my husband in Delhi.

Styling

When it comes to styling, it often works to make little or no effort at all. With a stunning backdrop like this, you can keep everything else simple. Scatter some old cushions and rugs on the sand, and serve the food on wooden chopping boards or wrapped up in butcher's paper, along with disposable wooden cutlery for that authentic seaside feel.

Playlist

Iron and Wine — Our Endless Numbered Days
Angus & Julia Stone — A Book Like This
Nick Drake — Bryter Layter
Kings of Convenience — Riot on an Empty Street
Neil Young — On the Beach

Menu

Lunch
Peach and Ginger Punch
Herb Chips
Crab Burgers
  served with
Chilli Relish & Aioli

Afternoon Tea
Indian Chai Tea
Vanilla Slices
Lamingtons

99

Peach and Ginger Punch

This refreshingly zingy punch is the perfect summertime drink. Make it the day before and keep it in the fridge overnight to allow the flavours to infuse.

750 ml sparkling wine
500 g sugar
200 g ginger, grated
1 sprig thyme
½ bunch mint
½ bunch basil
6 yellow peaches
6 limes, cut into wedges
soda water, to serve

Combine the wine, 250 ml (1 cup) of water, sugar, ginger, thyme and 1 sprig each of mint and basil in a medium saucepan with a lid. Bring to the boil, then turn the heat down to low and simmer.

Cut 4 peaches in half (reserving 2 to serve) and place in the liquid. Let the peaches gently simmer for 1 hour, stirring occasionally. (Be careful not to let the mixture boil.)

Remove the saucepan from the heat and allow the liquid to cool completely. Cover with a lid and place in the fridge overnight.

The next day, strain the syrup through a fine sieve into a serving jug. Cut the 2 reserved peaches into rough chunks and add to the punch along with the lime wedges, remaining basil and mint leaves, and plenty of ice.

To serve, top with a little soda water and give a quick stir to combine.

Serves 6 (with seconds)

Herb Chips

Nothing beats hot chips wrapped up in paper when you're at the seaside. Serve with dollops of homemade chilli relish and aioli (see recipes on the following page), if you like.

1 kg kipfler potatoes
sea salt
vegetable oil, for deep-frying
12 cloves garlic, unpeeled
½ bunch sage, leaves picked
½ bunch rosemary, sprigs separated
½ bunch parsley, leaves picked
1 red chilli, seeded and finely chopped
lemon wedges, to serve

Place the potatoes in a large saucepan and cover with cold water and a small handful of salt. Bring to the boil, then reduce heat and simmer for 20 minutes or until the potatoes are just cooked (pierce with a knife to test). Strain the pan and allow the potatoes to cool completely, then break them up with your hands.

Pour the oil into a large heavy-based saucepan until it is about two-thirds full. Heat the oil until it reaches 180°C. (To check the temperature without a thermometer, drop a cube of bread into the oil. The bread will brown in about 15 seconds if the oil is hot enough.) Working in batches, deep-fry the potatoes for 2 minutes, then lift out using a slotted spoon and drain on paper towel. Repeat until all of the potatoes are cooked.

Add the garlic cloves to the oil. Deep-fry for 30 seconds, then lift out using a slotted spoon and drain on paper towel. Very quickly and carefully, drop in the herbs and chilli (beware of spitting oil), then scoop out straight away and drain.

Transfer the chips to a bowl and scatter with garlic, herbs, chilli and a generous sprinkle of salt. Serve on butcher's paper with lemon wedges to squeeze over.

Serves 6

Summer Storm

Crab Burgers

I have to admit I love a good burger and they don't come much better than this one. Store the aioli in an airtight container in the fridge for up to 4–5 days; the chilli relish will keep for up to 1 month.

8 soft-shell crabs (approx 120 g each)
1 large eggplant (aubergine), thinly sliced
sea salt and freshly ground black pepper
vegetable oil, for deep-frying
1 large sweet potato or kumara,
    peeled and thinly sliced
200 g cornflour
cold soda water
6 bread rolls
2 avocados, thinly sliced
½ iceberg lettuce, leaves shredded
250 g rocket

Clean the crabs by cutting them in half and scooping out the mustard-coloured innards with a teaspoon. Set the crabs aside on paper towel.

Sprinkle the eggplant with a little salt and set aside for 30 minutes. Pat dry with paper towel.

Pour the oil into a large heavy-based saucepan until it is two-thirds full. Heat the oil until it reaches 180°C. (To check the temperature without a thermometer, drop a cube of bread into the oil. The bread will brown in about 15 seconds if the oil is hot enough.) Deep-fry the eggplant, turning the slices over, for 2 minutes or until golden brown and crisp. Drain on paper towel. Repeat with the sweet potato.

Place the cornflour in a bowl and use a fork to slowly mix in the soda water, adding just enough for a thin batter consistency. Coat the crabs in the batter and deep-fry, two at a time, for 1 minute or until crispy. Drain on paper towel.

Fill the bread rolls with the eggplant, sweet potato, crab, avocado and salad leaves.

Serve the burgers with generous dollops of chilli relish and aioli.

Serves 6

Chilli Relish

1 tablespoon olive oil
1 onion, finely chopped
3 cloves garlic, finely chopped
½ eggplant (aubergine), roughly chopped
80 ml (⅓ cup) red-wine vinegar
2 tablespoons sugar
2 long green chillies, finely chopped
2 long red chillies, finely chopped
½ teaspoon fennel seeds, toasted
½ teaspoon coriander seeds, toasted
250 g cherry tomatoes (ideally some red
    and some green), halved
sea salt and freshly ground black pepper

Heat the olive oil in a small saucepan over low heat. Add the onion and garlic, and fry until soft. Add the eggplant and cook for a further 5 minutes.

Add the red-wine vinegar and sugar, and simmer until the liquid has reduced by half. Add the chilli, fennel, coriander and tomato, and cook over very low heat, stirring occasionally, for about 30 minutes. Season with salt and pepper, to taste. Allow to cool before serving.

Makes 300 g (1½ cups)

Aioli

12 cloves garlic, peeled
50 ml extra virgin olive oil
1 egg
2 egg yolks
1 teaspoon mustard
1 tablespoon white-wine vinegar
200 ml vegetable oil
1 bunch chives, finely chopped
5 sprigs parsley, finely chopped
sea salt and freshly ground black pepper

Preheat the oven to 160°C. Wrap the garlic cloves in foil with a splash of olive oil and roast in the oven for 20–30 minutes or until really soft.

Place the roasted garlic in a bowl and mash with a fork. Add the egg, egg yolks, mustard and vinegar, and whisk to combine. Keep whisking while very slowly pouring in the vegetable oil, until the mixture is quite thick and creamy (this could take a few minutes). Whisk in the remaining olive oil. If the aioli is too thick, add a little hot water to thin.

Add the chives and parsley, and season with salt and pepper.

Makes 250 g (1 cup)

Indian Chai Tea

Living in India for two years really gave me a taste for chai. This recipe is authentic but not too intoxicating. Be generous with the sugar – this is meant to be sweet.

750 ml (3 cups) milk
60 ml (¼ cup) black tea
3 cloves
3 cardamom pods, crushed
1.5 cm piece ginger, peeled and finely sliced
1 cinnamon stick
sugar, to taste

Place the milk, tea and spices in a medium saucepan. Add 750 ml (3 cups) of water. Boil for 3–4 minutes, then remove from the heat. Add sugar to taste. Strain the chai and pour into glasses, to serve.

Serves 6

Vanilla Slices

These gooey pastries always remind me of childhood trips to the beach.

250 ml (1 cup) milk
250 ml (1 cup) cream
1 vanilla bean, split and seeds scraped (bean reserved)
7 egg yolks
50 g (⅓ cup) cornflour, sifted
180 g sugar
1 sheet titanium-strength gelatine
2 sheets ready-rolled puff pastry
200 g icing sugar
3 passionfruit, pulp removed

For the filling, heat the milk, cream and vanilla bean in a saucepan over high heat, watching carefully, until the mixture just begins to boil. Meanwhile, place the vanilla seeds in a large bowl with the egg yolks, cornflour and sugar. Whisk for 2 minutes until pale. Pour the hot cream into the egg mixture, stirring as you go. Transfer to a clean saucepan over very low heat and stir continuously with a spatula or wooden spoon for 10 minutes or until the mixture thickens and coats the spoon. Soften the gelatine in a little cold water, then squeeze out the excess liquid and mix into the custard. Using a fine sieve, strain the custard into a container and cool in the fridge until firm.

Preheat the oven to 200°C. Line a baking tray with baking paper. Place one sheet of pastry directly on top of the other and cut into 6 rectangles. Place on the prepared tray and bake for 10–15 minutes or until golden brown and puffed up.

Place the icing sugar in a bowl and add just enough hot water to form a smooth, thick paste. Stir through the passionfruit pulp. To assemble, cut the pastries in half and spoon the custard onto the bottom half. Top with the remaining pastry and decorate with passionfruit icing.

Makes 6

Lamingtons

An Aussie icon poshed up with freshly grated coconut, berries and whipped cream. Make the sponge the day before to allow it to dry out – it will be much easier to handle.

180 g dark chocolate, broken into small chunks
180 ml cream
1 coconut
1 punnet berries of your choice

Sponge
150 g (1 cup) plain flour
90 g cornflour
1½ teaspoons baking powder
pinch of salt
3 eggs
4 egg yolks
200 g caster sugar
50 ml white wine

Preheat the oven to 160°C. Lightly grease a small–medium cake tin.

For the sponge, sift the flour, cornflour, baking powder and salt into a large bowl. Combine the eggs, yolks, sugar and wine in a large heatproof bowl. Place the egg mixture over a saucepan of gently simmering water (making sure the bottom of the bowl does not touch the water), and whisk for 5–10 minutes or until a soft peak forms. Remove the bowl from the heat and gently fold in the flour mixture until well combined. Transfer the sponge mixture to the prepared cake tin and bake for 20–30 minutes or until firm.

Crack open the coconut and prise out the flesh. Grate the coconut flesh into a bowl and set aside. Combine the chocolate and 100 ml of the cream in a separate heatproof bowl and place over a saucepan of gently simmering water (making sure the bottom of the bowl does not touch the water). Stir until the chocolate has melted and the mixture is well combined.

Using a bread knife, trim the edges off the sponge and cut into large cubes. Dip into the still-warm chocolate, coating all sides, then roll in the grated coconut. Transfer to a wire rack to dry. Repeat with the remaining sponge pieces.

Whip the remaining cream in a bowl. Slice the lamingtons in half and fill with the whipped cream and berries. Serve.

Makes 6–8

BRUNCH IN THE CITY

RELAX INTO THE WEEKEND WITH THIS DELICIOUSLY SIMPLE BRUNCH.

BRUNCH on the weekend is probably my favourite meal of the week, and I've always enjoyed serving up food as others wade through the papers or recover from the working week. If we're eating out, we often head to cafes in the city, but this time we decided to host breakfast at roof level — right in the midst of the warehouses of the garment district, the centre of Sydney's fashion industry.

As you can see, it's not that glamorous — high fashion can often be fairly low rent — and we continued with that theme by using milk crates as chairs, battered old crockery and a mis-match of props that were lying around the office. All very al fresco and ad hoc.

My nephew Asher hopes to do some modelling to help pay his way through uni so we got him together with a few of his fellow, aspiring models. All useful images for their 'books', the make-or-break portfolio of snap-shots that they present at castings.

The beauty of this breakfast is its simplicity. You can prepare virtually all of it before your guests turn up. The baked eggs can sit in the fridge until you are ready to put them in the oven. Likewise, the citrus-poached fruit is something you can prepare beforehand. The pancake torte sounds trickier, but again is easy — you just layer the pancakes, one on top of the other, with walnuts and chocolate-espresso syrup, for that extra mid-morning caffeine hit.

Rosco

Cate

Christina

Saxon

Zac

Melise

Crystal

Asher

Lindsay

MODEL-LING MUST SOMETIMES FEEL LIKE THE MOST UNGLAMOROUS OF JOBS. THERE ARE THE CASTING CALLS AND THE LONG HOURS AND THEN THERE IS THE ABSURDITY OF HAVING TO WEAR SWIMSUITS IN DEPTHS OF WINTER AND HEAVY COATS AT THE HEIGHT OF SUMMER. IT IS NOT ENOUGH TO BE BEAUTIFUL. SUCCESSFUL MODELS NEED TO HAVE THAT OFTEN UNDEFINABLE X FACTOR.

STYLING:

Stylistically, this is a bit of a free for all. We used milk crates, a battered sofa and an old coffee table. You should use whatever comes to hand. Serve the food on communal platters or just straight from the roasting tin. And make sure you have stacks of newspapers and magazines available for lazy weekend reading.

PLAYLIST: The Velvet Underground (Loaded), Johnny Cash (The Essential), Massive Attack (Blue Lines), David Bowie (Hunky Dory), Cowboy Junkies (the Trinity Session)

MENU

CHERRY SLUSHIE

CITRUS-POACHED FRUIT WITH CRUNCHY ALMOND YOGHURT

PASSIONFRUIT AND COCONUT MUFFINS

BAKED EGGS WITH HAM CROQUETTES, LEMON THYME MUSHROOMS AND ROASTED VINE-RIPENED TOMATOES

PANCAKE TORTE WITH ESPRESSO SYRUP AND MAPLE CANDIED WALNUTS

CHERRY SLUSHIE

I love this vibrant, grown-up slushie. You can use strawberries, watermelon or even canned lychees instead of cherries, if you like.

300 g frozen cherries
1 litre apple juice
70 g (¼ cup) yoghurt
6 cherries, to garnish

Combine the frozen cherries, apple juice and 2 large handfuls of ice in a blender and process until well combined. Divide between six glasses. Add a spoonful of yoghurt and a cherry, to garnish.

Serves 6

CITRUS-POACHED FRUIT WITH CRUNCHY ALMOND YOGHURT

Poaching your own fruit is easy. Flavour the poaching water by adding spices – try nutmeg or a stick of cinnamon – or use a different liquid such as cranberry juice.

220 g (1 cup) caster sugar
zest of 1 lime
3 plums, halved and stones removed
3 apricots, halved and stones removed
3 peaches, halved and stones removed
6 small pears, peeled
560 g (2 cups) vanilla yoghurt
60 g slivered almonds, toasted
1 small handful mint leaves

Place the sugar, lime zest and 1 litre of water in a large saucepan over medium heat and stir until the sugar dissolves. Add the fruit and gently simmer for 35 minutes or until tender. Transfer the fruit to a serving dish, discarding the syrup. Allow to cool.

Combine the yoghurt and almonds in a bowl. Garnish the fruit with mint leaves, and serve with the almond yoghurt alongside.

Serves 6

PASSIONFRUIT AND COCONUT MUFFINS

We baked these pretty little muffins using brioche tins, but you can also make them using standard muffin tins.

375 g (2½ cups) self-raising flour
1½ teaspoons baking powder
1 teaspoon ground cinnamon
pinch of salt
45 g (½ cup) desiccated coconut
2 eggs
170 g (¾ cup) caster sugar
110 g unsalted butter, melted
250 ml (1 cup) milk
8 passionfruit, pulp removed
2 tablespoons demerara sugar
30 g (½ cup) freshly shaved coconut

Preheat the oven to 180°C. Lightly grease eight large brioche or 125 ml (½ cup) capacity muffin tins and place them on a baking tray lined with baking paper.

Sift the flour, baking powder, cinnamon and salt into a large bowl, then stir through the desiccated coconut. In a separate bowl, whisk the eggs and sugar until creamy. Add the butter, milk and a third of the passionfruit pulp and mix well. Gently fold the flour mixture into the wet mixture until just combined. Spoon the mixture into the tins and sprinkle with demerara sugar.

Bake for 25–30 minutes or until a skewer inserted into the middle comes out clean. When cool enough to handle, turn the muffins out onto a wire rack.

Combine the remaining passionfruit pulp and the shaved coconut in a small bowl and generously spoon over the top of each muffin.

Makes 8

BAKED EGGS

Sometimes only a hearty cooked breakfast – eggs, tomatoes, mushrooms, the works – will do. This one is so simple to throw together. A note about the ham croquettes: if you can't find kaiserfleisch (a smoked and salted cut of pork), use pancetta or ham off the bone instead.

1 bunch rocket
375 ml (1½ cups) good-quality tomato sauce (passata)
6 eggs
120 ml (½ cup) pure cream
sea salt and cracked black pepper
sourdough toast, to serve

Preheat the oven to 180°C. Place six 250 ml (1 cup) capacity ramekins on a baking tray and line with the rocket. Divide the tomato sauce between the ramekins, then break an egg into each. Pour 1 tablespoon of cream over the top of each egg.

Bake the eggs for 10 minutes or until cooked through. Season well with salt and pepper.

Serve immediately with buttered sourdough toast, roasted tomatoes, mushrooms and ham croquettes.

Serves 6

ROASTED VINE-RIPENED TOMATOES

2 punnets vine-ripened cherry tomatoes
2 tablespoons olive oil
sea salt and cracked black pepper
1 small handful baby basil leaves

Preheat the oven to 180°C. Place the tomatoes on a baking tray and drizzle with the olive oil. Season with salt and pepper.

Roast the tomatoes for 20–25 minutes or until softened.

Toss with the baby basil leaves, to serve.

Serves 6

LEMON THYME MUSHROOMS

6 field mushrooms
20 g butter, finely chopped
8 sprigs lemon thyme, leaves picked
sea salt and cracked black pepper

Preheat the oven to 180°C. Place the mushrooms on a baking tray and top with the chopped butter and lemon thyme leaves. Season with salt and pepper.

Roast the mushrooms for 30 minutes or until tender.

Serves 6

HAM CROQUETTES

700 g (about 6) desiree potatoes,
    peeled and chopped
20 g butter
1 brown onion, finely chopped
200 g kaiserfleisch, finely chopped
3 tablespoons chopped parsley
sea salt and freshly cracked pepper
24 slices jamon
1 tablespoon vegetable oil

Place the potatoes in a saucepan and cover with water. Bring to the boil and simmer for 20 minutes or until tender. Drain, then return the potatoes to the pan. Mash until smooth.

Melt the butter in a frying pan, then add the onion and cook for 3–4 minutes or until slightly caramelised.

Add the onion, kaiserfleisch and parsley to the mashed potato, season with salt and pepper, and mix well. Take handfuls of the mixture and mould into 24 croquettes, each about 2.5 cm × 5 cm.

Wrap each croquette with a slice of jamon. Refrigerate until ready to cook.

Heat the oil in a large frying pan over medium heat. Cook the croquettes, in batches, for 3–4 minutes on each side or until golden all over.

Serves 6

PANCAKE TORTE WITH ESPRESSO SYRUP AND MAPLE CANDIED WALNUTS

**Chocolate, caffeine and cream (and that's just the sauce).
Go on, indulge. It's the weekend.**

300 g (2 cups) plain flour
pinch of salt
1 teaspoon bicarbonate of soda
3 eggs, separated
500 ml (2 cups) buttermilk
60 g butter, melted
canola oil spray, for greasing

Maple candied walnuts
60 ml (¼ cup) maple syrup
100 g walnut halves

Espresso syrup
2 tablespoons espresso coffee
250 ml (1 cup) pure cream
150 g good-quality dark chocolate, chopped

For the maple candied walnuts, heat a small frying pan over medium heat. Add the maple syrup and bring to a simmer. Add the walnuts and toss to coat. Cook for 2–3 minutes or until the walnuts are completely coated. Transfer to a baking tray lined with baking paper and allow to cool.

For the espresso syrup, combine the coffee with 60 ml (¼ cup) of cream in a small bowl. Place the remaining cream and the chocolate in a saucepan over medium heat and stir until the chocolate melts. Stir in the coffee mixture and set aside until required.

Sift the flour, salt and bicarbonate of soda into a large bowl. In a separate bowl, combine the egg yolks, buttermilk and butter, and whisk well. Add to the flour and stir to combine. Place the egg whites in a clean, dry glass bowl and whisk to soft peaks. Fold the egg whites through the batter.

Heat a non-stick frying pan over medium heat and lightly spray with oil. Add 3 tablespoons of batter to the pan and cook the pancakes for 1–2 minutes on each side until golden. Transfer the pancakes to a baking tray and cover with foil to keep warm. Repeat with the remaining batter.

To serve, gently reheat the espresso syrup. Place a pancake on a serving platter and spread with 1 tablespoon of the syrup, then sprinkle over 1 teaspoon of maple candied walnuts. Continue to layer, alternating pancakes, syrup and walnuts. Finish by spooning over the remaining espresso syrup and walnuts.

Serves 6

HIGH FASHION CAN BE VERY LOW RENT. (AND IT IS NEVER AS GLAMOROUS AS IT SEEMS.)

2678

Anne Marie Kelly

MU
RI

18 43

IN THE MID-NINETEENTH CENTURY,
MY GREAT, GREAT, GREAT GRANDMOTHER
SAILED ACROSS THE SEAS
FROM ENGLAND TO NEW ZEALAND.
THIS DINNER IS INSPIRED
BY HER AMAZING JOURNEY:
ENTER DELICATE VICTORIAN LACE,
BILLOWING SAILS, EXQUISITE URCHINS
AND SEASHELL PASTA.

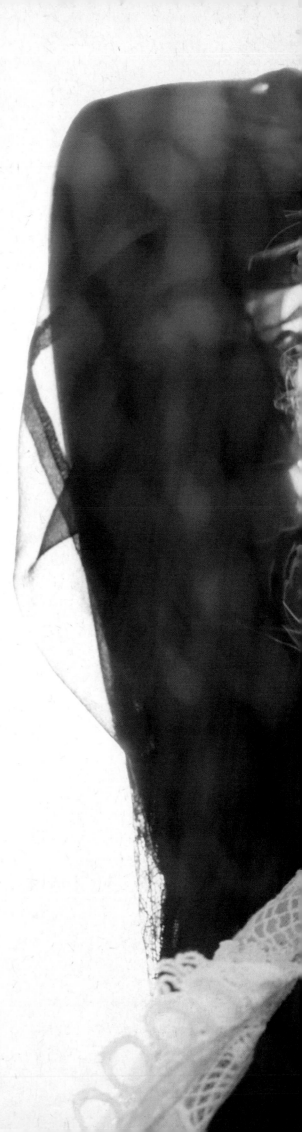

1843 is the year that my great, great, great grandmother, Mary Ann Hodgkinson, ended an epic voyage from England to New Zealand. Fortunately, she left behind a journal from that perilous journey – a real treasure trove of tales and adventures. She came ashore dressed in crinoline, with flowers in her bonnet, and looked on in horror as she saw 'a dark tattooed Maori advancing violently toward me with a club'. But the Maori warrior burst into laughter, and Mary Ann and her husband soon realised they were actually being welcomed rather than attacked. 'No kinder folk ever existed on this earth,' she later wrote.

The journal tells of how she planted cherry plums and laurel stones to make ointments, travelled the Pacific Islands collecting flora and fauna, and sold beautiful lace shawls at the Wellington markets – my family's first start in the fashion business, I guess. Mary Ann was obviously a remarkably adventurous and independent woman, so we decided to adopt her as our muse for the Winter 2009 collection. The influences from Victorian England and the Pacific Islands come through in the use of the delicate laces and shells.

To launch the collection, we hosted a sit-down dinner for key fashion writers and buyers in my studio. Wanting to recreate the look and feel of Mary Ann's amazing voyage, we draped thirty huge sails from the roof of the studio – real, authentic sails that we got from a local shipyard. We added layers of black Chantilly lace to the dinner tables and loaded them up with piles of shells and candles. I still think one of the simplest but prettiest touches of the night was the sea urchin shells threaded with fairy lights that ran down the middle of the table. Beautiful.

For the food, I turned to one of my favourite neighbourhood restaurants, Vini, which is just around the corner from the studio in Sydney. Dan, the chef, did a fabulous job of interpreting our theme. Referencing the seashell prints in the collection, he came up with seashell pasta for the menu. We used New Zealand fish but, at the same time, tried to avoid overcooking the Kiwi theme. We catered for forty that night, but the menu would have worked just as well for six.

Mary Ann talks in her journal about eating some pretty unappetising porridge. I promise these recipes will be much more flavoursome.

SET THE SCENE

STYLING
FOR THE TABLE

A white tablecloth
Black Chantilly lace
Sea urchin shells threaded
  with strings of fairy lights
Sea shells of assorted sizes
Glass vases filled with pink,
  purple and white flowers
  (we used flannel flowers,
  hydrangeas and orchids)
  and greenery
White candles and silver candlesticks
White napkins tied with black ribbon

PLAYLIST

Geoffrey Gurrumul Yunupingu *GURRUMUL*
Claudine Longet *COLOURS*
Hellsongs *HYMNS IN THE KEY OF 666*
Nossa Alma Canta *I WAS MADE FOR BOSSA*
Nina Simone *GOLD*

MENU

To Start

CROSTINI WITH
Seared tuna, olives and chives
Marinated capsicum, roast almonds and mint
Buffalo mozzarella, smoked eggplant and pancetta

Entree

CONCHIGLIONE WITH GOAT'S CHEESE,
PRESERVED LEMON AND FRESH PEAS

Main

SNAPPER AL CARTOCCIO

Dessert

RICOTTA PANNA COTTA WITH ESPRESSO CARAMEL

To Start
Crostini

I always seem to be hungry the moment I arrive at a dinner party. So when I host my own event, I like to make sure that my guests have a selection of delicious hors d'œuvre to nibble on before the main meal.

1 baguette, sliced into 18 thin pieces

Preheat the oven to 140°C. Spread out the baguette slices on a baking tray and bake until crisp.

To serve, add the following toppings:

Seared tuna, olives and chives

200 g yellowfin tuna, mid loin, sinew and bloodline removed
sea salt and freshly ground black pepper
1 tablespoon olive oil
50 g kalamata olives, pitted and very finely chopped
1 clove garlic, very finely chopped
½ lemon
extra virgin olive oil, for drizzling
½ bunch chives, finely chopped

Season the tuna with salt and pepper. Heat the olive oil in a frying pan over medium heat. Sear the tuna for about 10 seconds on each side or until lightly coloured. (The heat should only penetrate a few millimetres of the flesh.) Allow to cool, then slice into six pieces.

Meanwhile, mix together the olives and garlic. Add a squeeze of lemon and a drizzle of extra virgin olive oil.

Spread the olive mixture over six crostini. Top with a slice of tuna and sprinkle with chives.

Marinated capsicum, roast almonds and mint

2 red capsicums (peppers)
olive oil, for roasting
50 g almonds
1 clove garlic, finely chopped
1 sprig mint, finely chopped
1 tablespoon extra virgin olive oil
1 tablespoon balsamic vinegar
sea salt and freshly ground black pepper

Preheat the oven to 220°C. Rub the capsicums all over with a little olive oil and roast in the oven, turning occasionally, for 20 minutes or until the skin is thoroughly blistered. Place in a bowl, cover with plastic film and set aside until cool.

Reduce the oven temperature to 150°C. Spread the almonds on a baking tray and roast in the oven, stirring frequently, for about 20 minutes or until the nuts are light brown inside when broken. Allow to cool, then roughly chop.

Once the capsicum is cool, peel the skin, discard the seeds and cut into strips. Combine with the garlic, mint, extra virgin olive oil and balsamic vinegar, then season with salt and pepper.

Spoon the capsicum mixture over six crostini and top with a few chopped almonds.

Buffalo mozzarella, smoked eggplant and pancetta

1 large eggplant (aubergine)
1 clove garlic, finely chopped
2 sprigs parsley, finely chopped
1 tablespoon extra virgin olive oil
sea salt and freshly ground black pepper
6 slices pancetta
200 g buffalo mozzarella, sliced

Heat a barbecue grill or grill pan over high heat. Place the eggplant onto the grill and cook for 10 minutes or until blackened on one side, then turn to blacken all sides. (The flesh of the eggplant should be very soft and smoky.) Allow to cool, then scoop out the flesh and mix with the garlic, parsley and olive oil. Season with salt and pepper.

Preheat the oven to 160°C. Lay the pancetta slices on a baking tray and bake until crisp.

Spoon the eggplant mixture over six crostini. Add a slice of seasoned mozzarella and top with a piece of crisp pancetta.

Serves 6

CONCHIGLIONE WITH GOAT'S CHEESE, PRESERVED LEMON AND FRESH PEAS

Half-cooking pasta may be regarded as sacrilege by some,
but it is necessary for this recipe.

400 g conchiglione (large pasta shells)
2 tablespoons olive oil
1 leek, finely chopped
1 onion, finely chopped
2 cloves garlic, finely chopped
300 g goat's cheese
120 g ricotta
3 sprigs thyme, chopped
handful grated parmesan
1 preserved lemon wedge, flesh discarded, thinly sliced
sea salt and freshly ground black pepper
1 × 400 g can chopped tomatoes
250 ml (1 cup) chicken stock
2 sprigs basil
150 g fresh peas

Cook the pasta in plenty of salted, boiling water until half cooked (about 3–4 minutes). Strain, then rinse under cold water.

Heat 1 tablespoon of olive oil in a frying pan over medium heat and gently saute the leek, onion and garlic for 15 minutes or until very soft. Allow to cool. In a large bowl, combine the goat's cheese and ricotta. Add the leek mixture, thyme, parmesan and preserved lemon. Season well.

Preheat the oven to 180°C. Pour the tomato into a baking dish. Add half of the stock and a couple of basil leaves, and season with salt and pepper. Fill the pasta shells by carefully spooning in the goat's cheese mixture. Place in the baking dish. Once all shells are in (about 3 per serve), add a drizzle of olive oil and enough stock to come about halfway up the sides of the shells. Cover with foil and bake for about 20 minutes or until the pasta is cooked through.

Blanch the peas in salted, boiling water. Strain, then toss with basil, olive oil and a little salt. Arrange the stuffed shells and sauce on serving plates and spoon over the peas. Serve.

Serves 6

Main

Snapper al cartoccio

Cooking al cartoccio ('in paper') is a great way to seal in flavour.
Unwrap the parcels at the table and drink in the gorgeous
citrus and marjoram aromas as they're released.

2 large desiree potatoes, thinly sliced
finely grated zest and juice of 1 lemon
1 long red chilli, finely sliced
½ bunch marjoram, finely chopped
2 tablespoons extra virgin olive oil
sea salt and freshly ground black pepper
6 × 150 g skinless snapper fillets
12 zucchini (courgette) flowers

Cook the potatoes in a large saucepan of salted, boiling water for 2–3 minutes or until al dente, then strain. Combine the lemon zest, 1 tablespoon of lemon juice, chilli, marjoram and a tablespoon of olive oil in a bowl, season with salt and pepper, and drizzle over the potatoes.

Preheat the oven to 180°C. Cut baking paper into six pieces approximately 35 cm × 25 cm. Place a few potato slices in the middle of each. Season the fish with salt and pepper, and then place on the potato. Top with 2 zucchini flowers. Drizzle with a little olive oil and a touch more lemon juice. Fold the two long edges together and roll down, tucking the flaps underneath to make a parcel. Bake on a tray in the oven for 12 minutes or until the fish is just cooked.

Serve straight away, as the contents of the parcel will keep cooking inside the bag.

Serves 6

18
43

PREŞEDINTE

RICOTTA PANNA COTTA WITH ESPRESSO CARAMEL

Vini is famous for its panna cotta. You'll need to start this
the day before to allow it to set overnight.

3 sheets gelatine
260 ml cream
100 g honey
400 g ricotta
260 ml milk
200 g caster sugar
100 ml strong espresso coffee
100 g roasted almonds, roughly chopped

Soften the gelatine in cold water and squeeze out any excess liquid. Heat the cream and honey in a saucepan over medium heat until almost boiling, then add the gelatine and stir to dissolve. Remove from the heat.

Using a hand-held blender, combine the ricotta and milk in a large bowl. Stir in the cream mixture. Using a fine sieve, strain into six 125 ml (½ cup) capacity moulds and set in the fridge overnight.

Bring the sugar and 50 ml of water to the boil and heat until a deep caramel colour. Quickly and carefully, stir in the coffee. Bring back to the boil for 1 minute, then remove from the heat and allow to cool completely.

Turn out the panna cotta onto serving plates. Generously douse with the caramel and top with chopped roasted almonds.

Serves 6

I love dim lighting.
It creates a mood of intimacy,
no matter how many guests there are.

Found objects and hand-me-downs
add sentimental value -
and they always look great.

When I am styling an event,
I always like to mix the unexpected,
like seashells and Chantilly lace.

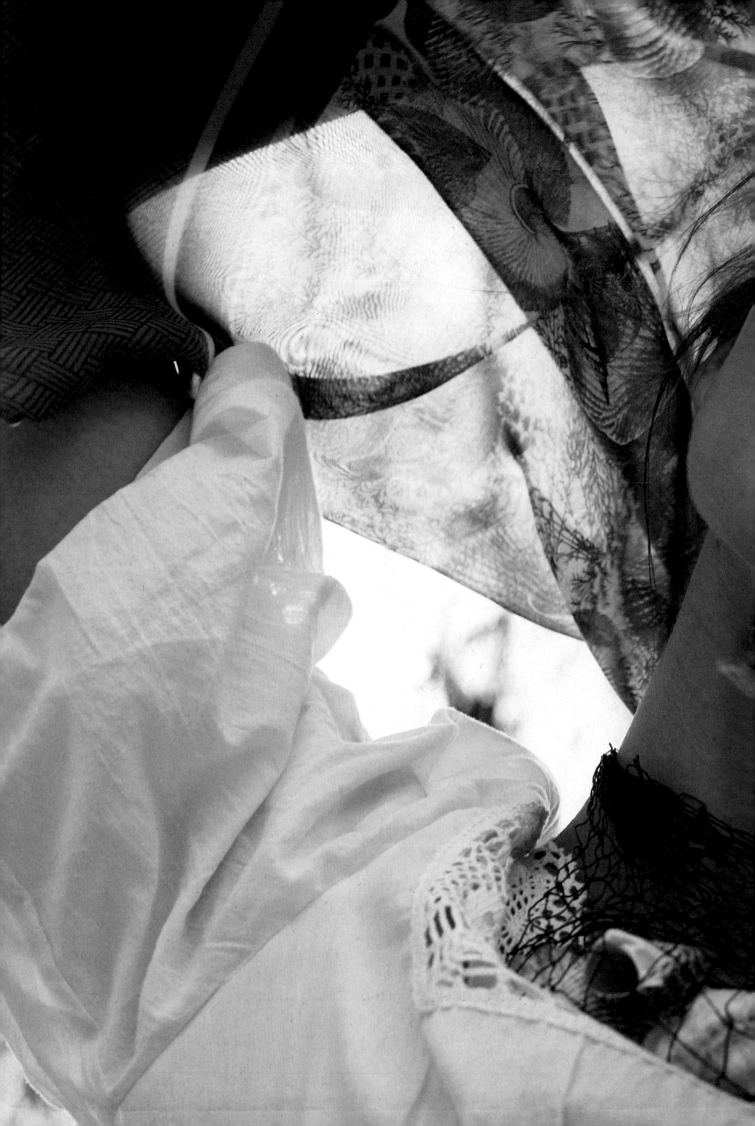

A WEEKEND IN THE COUNTRY

PULL ON YOUR WELLIES,
PACK UP THE HAMPER,
AND ESCAPE TO THE ROLLING HILLS
FOR A COUNTRYSIDE PICNIC.
(MENAGERIE OF ANIMALS AND
300 BALLOONS OPTIONAL.)

FOR THIS COUNTRY PICNIC, WE HEADED TO THE FRINGES OF THE SOUTHERN HIGHLANDS, SOUTH OF SYDNEY. IT WAS A BIRTHDAY CELEBRATION FOR MY HUSBAND, NICK, AND THE LANDSCAPE OFFERED THE MOST PERFECT OF BACKDROPS.

Nick is British, a foreign correspondent with the BBC, and the rolling hills remind him of where he grew up in the West Country. To make him feel even more at home, we invited some of his British friends who have come to live in Australia. They were more than happy to embrace the countryside theme and arrived looking like they were to the manor born.

They say you should never work with children and animals, but the cows were on their best behaviour, as was Skip, our labrador, and his new best friend, the local farmyard dog. They make for a pretty photogenic menagerie of animals. The beautiful girl in many of the photos is Lauren, who looks like she could have come straight from the set of one of those British period dramas.

The food is super-simple and fuss-free. Everything is easy to prepare and transport, and most of the dishes can be made the day before. The picnic bread is even tastier if the flavours are left to develop overnight. And, even if I say so myself, the iced chocolate cookies are to die for. Dark, rich and delicious, they are especially close to my heart because they remind me of the cookies my mum made for me as a kid.

This being a birthday, we needed balloons. Hundreds of them, in fact. Bursting them all at the end was all part of the fun, and made sure that Nick's countryside birthday ended with the requisite bang.

SET THE SCENE

STYLING

Hundreds of balloons
Picnic blankets and cushions
  (and old tables and chairs, if you like)
Wicker hampers
A mix of old enamelware and china
Vintage glasses and pitchers
A cake stand and large wooden trays
A blackboard, to scribble birthday wishes
  (or whatever takes your fancy)
Dogs, cows and kids (optional)

PLAYLIST

Van Morrison *Astral Weeks*
Crosby, Stills, Nash & Young *Déjà Vu*
The Beatles *Abbey Road*
Goldfrapp *Seventh Tree*
Fleet Foxes *Fleet Foxes*

MENU

FRESH LEMONADE WITH BLACKBERRIES

SOMETHING SAVOURY

BLOOD ORANGE, RADICCHIO AND FRISEE SALAD
WITH ORANGE BLOSSOM DRESSING

PORK SAUSAGE BUNS WITH RED PLUM RELISH

PICNIC BREAD WITH CHEDDAR AND BABY FIGS

MACADAMIA AND LEMON FRIED CHICKEN

ROASTED POTATO SALAD WITH
PRESERVED LEMON AND FRESH HERBS

SOMETHING SWEET

ICED CHOCOLATE COOKIES

MARBLE CAKES

JAM TART WITH BERRIES

FRESH LEMONADE WITH BLACKBERRIES

Nothing beats fresh lemonade for a refreshing summer drink. Drop the blackberries in at the last minute and watch the pretty purple colour appear.

250 ml (1 cup) lemon juice (approx 8 lemons)
220 g (1 cup) caster sugar
1 litre soda water
1 × 225 g punnet blackberries

Combine the lemon juice, caster sugar and soda water in a large jug and mix well until the sugar dissolves.

To serve, drop in the blackberries and pour into tall glasses.

Serves 6

BLOOD ORANGE, RADICCHIO AND FRISEE SALAD WITH ORANGE BLOSSOM DRESSING

This is a beautifully fresh and vibrant salad. If blood oranges are not in season, you can use any stone fruit or grapes instead. Keep the dressing in a jar and drizzle over the salad just before serving.

4 small blood oranges, peeled and sliced
1 bunch small frisee, separated
2 small radicchio, leaves separated
1 small red onion, thinly sliced
sea salt and cracked black pepper

Orange blossom dressing
3 tablespoons orange blossom water
(available from good delis)
1 tablespoon white balsamic vinegar
(available from good delis)
1 tablespoon caster sugar
3 tablespoons olive oil

Combine the dressing ingredients in a small screw-top jar and shake well until combined.

To serve, combine the salad ingredients in a bowl, pour over the dressing and season with salt and pepper.

Serves 6

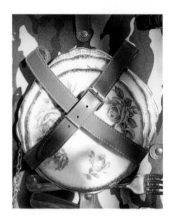

PORK SAUSAGE BUNS WITH RED PLUM RELISH

A delicious take on the good old sausage sandwich.
The red plum relish is great with cheese and cold meats, too.

1 tablespoon olive oil
6 fat pork sausages
6 bread rolls

Red plum relish
1 × 825 g can whole plums, drained,
seeds removed and juice discarded
1 star anise
1 clove garlic, crushed
2 tablespoons brown sugar
2 tablespoons red-wine vinegar
¼ teaspoon ground mustard
sea salt

For the red plum relish, combine the plums, star anise, garlic, sugar, vinegar and mustard in a medium saucepan over medium heat. Simmer for 40 minutes or until the relish is thick. Season with sea salt and allow to cool.

Heat the olive oil in a saucepan over medium heat. Cook the sausages for 3–4 minutes on each side, turning until cooked through.

Cut the sausages to fit into the buns. Add a dollop of red plum relish, and serve.

Serves 6

PICNIC BREAD WITH CHEDDAR AND BABY FIGS

Perfect picnic food – hearty and wholesome, and easy
to transport. We used sweet marinated baby figs,
which you can find in delis and farmers' markets;
if you can't get hold of them, sliced salami works well.
Make this the day before to allow the flavours to combine.

1 × 20 cm round loaf
100 g fig paste
200 g soft cheddar, sliced
100 g pickled onions, sliced
100 g sweet marinated baby figs, halved
1 small handful mixed green leaves

Using a small sharp knife, cut a 15 cm circle from the top of the loaf. Pull out as much bread as you can, leaving at least a 2 cm border of bread inside the crust. (Reserve the top and insides of bread.)

Add the fillings in layers. Start with the fig paste, followed by the cheese, pickled onions, baby figs and mixed leaves. Press in a layer of bread and repeat with fillings. Continue this process until the loaf is filled. Press the lid back on top and wrap tightly in plastic film. Store in the fridge overnight.

Cut into wedges and serve.

Serves 6

MACADAMIA AND LEMON FRIED CHICKEN

I know fried chicken has a bad rap, but sometimes you just have to indulge. You can prepare this the day before your picnic. Simply allow the chicken to cool, then store in an airtight container in the fridge.

8 slices day-old white bread
grated zest of 2 lemons
100 g macadamias
sea salt and cracked black pepper
150 g (1 cup) plain flour
4 eggs, lightly whisked
1 × 1.6 kg organic chicken, cut into 10 pieces
1 litre vegetable oil
lemon wedges, to serve

Place the bread, lemon zest and macadamias in a food processor. Blend until well combined and the mixture resembles fine breadcrumbs. Transfer to a plate and season with salt and pepper.

Place the flour on one plate and the egg on another. Taking one piece at a time, coat the chicken in flour, then egg and finally the breadcrumbs. Set aside on another plate.

Heat the oil in a large heavy-based saucepan over medium heat until a small cube of bread sizzles in the hot oil. Carefully immerse the chicken in the oil and cook on each side for 4–5 minutes or until golden all over and cooked through.

Serve with lemon wedges.

Serves 6

ROASTED POTATO SALAD WITH PRESERVED LEMON AND FRESH HERBS

I am not usually a fan of cold potato, but this is really special. The trick is to use chat potatoes and to make sure they're over- rather than under-cooked. The roasted garlic in the mayo makes it all sweet and caramely.

2 tablespoons olive oil
2 kg chat potatoes, halved
1 bulb of garlic
sea salt and cracked black pepper
300 g (1 cup) high-quality whole egg mayonnaise
2 tablespoons lemon juice
2 tablespoons chopped chives
1 large handful parsley leaves, chopped
1 small handful mint leaves, chopped
1 preserved lemon wedge, flesh discarded, finely chopped

Preheat the oven to 180°C. Combine the olive oil, potato and garlic in a large bowl and season with salt and pepper. Turn the potatoes and garlic bulb out onto a baking tray. Roast for 20–25 minutes or until golden and cooked through. Allow to cool.

Remove the garlic from the bulb by squeezing the bottom of each clove until the soft roasted garlic pops free. Combine the mayonnaise, garlic and lemon juice in a small bowl, then season and set aside.

Place the cooled potato, mayonnaise, herbs and preserved lemon in a large bowl. Mix well just before serving.

Serves 6

ICED CHOCOLATE COOKIES

This is my version of the cookies Mum made
for me as a kid. So simple and so scrumptious.

400 g butter, softened
220 g (1 cup) brown sugar
375 g (2½ cups) plain flour
4 tablespoons cocoa

Icing
320 g (2 cups) icing sugar
2 tablespoons cocoa
2 tablespoons boiling water

Preheat the oven to 180°C. Line two baking trays with baking paper.

Cream the butter and sugar until light and fluffy. Sift the flour and
cocoa into a bowl and stir into the butter mixture until well combined.

Roughly roll a handful of cookie dough into a ball and use the palm
of your hand to flatten it on the baking tray. Repeat with remaining
cookie dough.

Bake the cookies for 15 minutes or until set. Allow to cool, then
transfer to a wire rack.

For the icing, sift together the icing sugar and cocoa, and mix with
boiling water until smooth. Use a butter knife to spread the icing
evenly over each cookie. (Add as much or as little as you like.)

Makes 10

MARBLE CAKES

These rainbow-coloured cakes dribbled with icing
are almost too pretty to eat.

150 g (1 cup) self-raising flour
150 g (1 cup) plain flour
200 g butter
220 g (1 cup) caster sugar
1 teaspoon vanilla essence
3 eggs
125 ml (½ cup) milk
2 teaspoons red food colouring
2 tablespoons cocoa, sifted

Lemon icing
160 g (1 cup) icing sugar, sifted
1 tablespoon lemon juice

Preheat the oven to 180°C. Lightly grease nine 125 ml (½ cup)
capacity bundt tins.

Sift the flours into a bowl. In a separate medium glass bowl, combine
the butter, sugar and vanilla, and beat with an electric mixer until pale
and creamy. Add the eggs one at a time, beating after each addition.
Alternately fold in the flour mixture and the milk until well combined.

Divide the cake mixture between three bowls. Add the red food
colouring to one and the cocoa to another. Stir to mix through.
Spoon equal measures of all three cake mixtures into each bundt tin
and swirl together with a skewer. Bake for 30–35 minutes or until
a skewer inserted into the middle comes out clean. Allow to cool
slightly, then turn out onto a wire rack.

For the lemon icing, combine the icing sugar, lemon juice and
1–2 tablespoons water in a small bowl and mix until smooth. Spoon
the icing over the bundt cakes, allowing it to run down the sides.

Makes 9

JAM TART WITH BERRIES

Jam tart and the countryside just seem to be the perfect match.

1 sheet titanium-strength gelatine
1.1 kg raspberry jam
1 × 250 g punnet strawberries, hulled and halved
1 × 125 g punnet raspberries
1 × 125 g punnet blueberries
1 tablespoon icing sugar, for dusting

Pastry
125 g plain flour
70 g chilled unsalted butter, finely chopped
55 g (¼ cup) caster sugar
pinch of salt
2 egg yolks
2 teaspoons iced water

For the pastry, process the flour, butter, sugar and salt in a food processor until the mixture resembles breadcrumbs. Mix 1 egg yolk with the iced water, add to the crumbs and process until the mixture just comes together. Form the dough into a flat rectangle, then wrap in plastic film and refrigerate for 1 hour.

Remove the pastry from the fridge and roll out between two sheets of lightly floured baking paper. Line an 11 cm × 34 cm tart tin (with a removable base) with the pastry. Cover and place in the freezer for 2 hours.

Preheat the oven to 180°C. Line the pastry with baking paper and fill with baking weights. Place on a baking tray and bake for 15 minutes. Remove the weights and paper, then bake for another 10 minutes or until dry and pale golden. Allow to cool. Lightly whisk the remaining egg yolk and evenly brush over the pastry to form a 'raincoat' for the wet jam mixture.

Soak the gelatine in cold water until soft, then squeeze out any excess water. Combine the jam and gelatine in a bowl and mix well, then spoon into the pastry base. Combine the berries in a separate bowl and evenly sprinkle over the top of the jam. Bake the tart for 10–15 minutes or until the berries have softened. Allow to cool completely before removing from the tart tin.

Dust the tart with icing sugar and cut into slices. Serve.

Serves 6

WHAT COULD BE MORE FUN THAN ORGANISING A SURPRISE FOR THE PEOPLE YOU LOVE?

WINTER SOLSTICE

CHASE AWAY THE CHILL WITH
A MAGICAL FONDUE FEAST.

The winter solstice, the shortest day of the year, is always worth celebrating because it is a reminder that summer is just over the horizon, and through the ages it has been marked with an extravagant feast. Admittedly, the normal temptation would be to head somewhere warm and snug, and to huddle around an open fire. But since time immemorial, solstices have been celebrated in the open air under brooding midwinter skies, so we decided to hold this dinner in the middle of the forest. The table and chairs were configured around the twisted roots of giant pines, while the light came from the moon, the stars, candles and a seventies disco ball hanging from the branches. As for heat, we decided to bring our own fire, which came courtesy of our flame juggler.

In Greek mythology, the winter solstice brings together a gathering of the Gods. But our guest list simply included a few good friends. Some of them wore masquerade masks to add to the sense of mysticism.

Like the disco ball, the food is something from the seventies that is well worth reviving: a fondue. There's a whole dining etiquette surrounding fondue — double dipping is a definite no no, for a start — along with a few sacrosanct traditions. If a morsel of food is lost in the cheese or chocolate by a man, he is expected to purchase a bottle of wine. If a woman commits the same mistake, she is expected to kiss the man to her left. So fondue for a winter festival: chase away the chill with this most communal of meals.

SET THE SCENE

STYLING
1 DISCO BALL
BLACK FABRIC, TO COVER CHAIRS
MASQUERADE MASKS (OPTIONAL)

FOR THE TABLE
A GREY TABLECLOTH
SILVER LACE
MOSS, LICHEN AND BUNCHES OF TWIGS
A CANDELABRUM OR TWO
WHITE CANDLES AND SILVER CANDLESTICKS
FONDUE SETS (SEE PAGE 201)

PLAYLIST
LEONARD COHEN *THE ESSENTIAL*
MIDLAKE *THE TRIALS OF VAN OCCUPANTHER*
PJ HARVEY *STORIES FROM THE CITY, STORIES FROM THE SEA*
THE ROLLING STONES *40 LICKS* OR *BEGGARS BANQUET*
NICK CAVE AND THE BAD SEEDS *THE BEST OF*

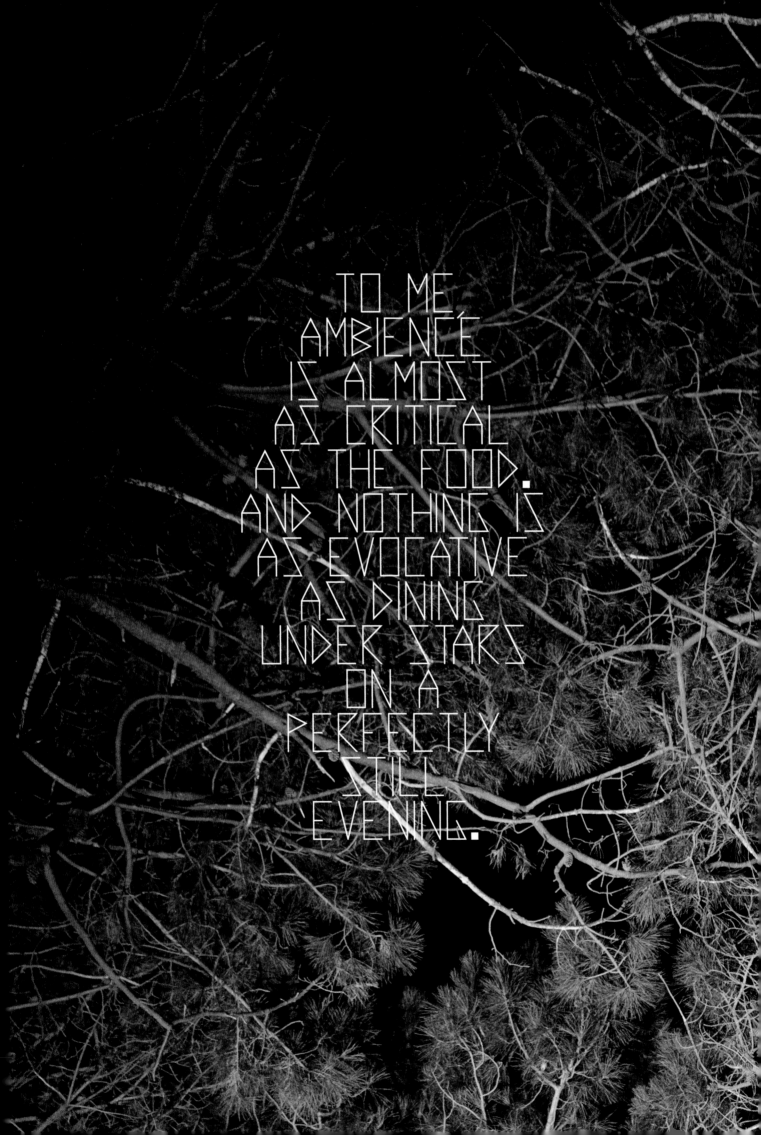

TO ME,
AMBIENCE
IS ALMOST
AS CRITICAL
AS THE FOOD.
AND NOTHING IS
AS EVOCATIVE
AS DINING
UNDER STARS
ON A
PERFECTLY
STILL
EVENING.

MENU

THREE-CHEESE FONDUE

WITH

FRESHLY SHUCKED OYSTERS
TORN BAGUETTE
STEAMED ASPARAGUS
CARAMELISED SHALLOTS

CHILLI OIL FONDUE

WITH

CRUMBED STUFFED OLIVES
BEEF WELLINGTON CROUTES
CHICKEN AND CAPER SKEWERS
SCALLOPS IN PROSCIUTTO

SPINACH AND HERB SALAD WITH
TRUFFLE OIL DRESSING

DARK CHOCOLATE SICHUAN FONDUE
ROSEWATER WHITE CHOCOLATE FONDUE

WITH

TURKISH DELIGHT
FIGS
HONEYCOMB

THE
SHORTEST
DAY HAS THE
LONGEST
NIGHT,
SO MAKE IT
ONE TO
REMEMBER.

THREE-CHEESE FONDUE

As the fondue cooks, a rich brown crust may form at the bottom of the fondue dish. Don't be alarmed – this is considered by some as the best part of the fondue.

1 clove garlic, cut in half
375 ml (1½ cups) white wine
300 g gruyere, grated
300 g tasty cheddar, grated
150 g blue cheese, crumbled
2 tablespoons cornflour
60 ml (¼ cup) kirsch

Rub the inside of a fondue pot with the cut garlic clove. Heat the wine in the pot over high heat until boiling. Reduce the heat to low. Add the cheese a handful at a time, stirring constantly and making sure it has melted before adding more.

Place the cornflour in a small bowl. Add the kirsch, stirring to form a slurry. Add the kirsch mixture to the cheese, stirring in a figure-of-eight motion until the mixture is smooth and slightly thickened. Keep warm over low heat, stirring occasionally to keep smooth.

Serves 6

FOR DIPPING

18–24 FRESHLY SHUCKED OYSTERS

1 BAGUETTE, TORN INTO SMALL PIECES

12 MIXED WHITE AND GREEN ASPARAGUS
    SPEARS, STEAMED

CARAMELISED SHALLOTS (SEE RECIPE OPPOSITE)

CARAMELISED SHALLOTS

1 tablespoon olive oil
1 tablespoon butter
350 g golden shallots, peeled
2 tablespoons balsamic vinegar
1 tablespoon brown sugar

Heat the oil and butter in a large frying pan with a lid over medium heat. Add the shallots and cook, stirring occasionally, for 5 minutes or until golden.

Add the vinegar and sugar, and stir to combine. Reduce the heat to low. Simmer, covered, for 15 minutes or until the shallots are caramelised.

Serves 6

CHILLI OIL FONDUE

Always use the right fondue equipment for your recipe. A ceramic pot is best for cheese and chocolate, while a stainless-steel or cast-iron pot is essential for hot oil. Look for a fondue set with adjustable temperature control. (Tea lights may be fine for cheese and chocolate, but won't provide enough heat for oil fondues.)

1 litre olive oil
4 small red chillies, chopped
large handful sage leaves

Heat the oil in a large heavy-based saucepan over medium heat, until a cube of bread sizzles on contact. Add the chilli and sage, and cook until crisp. Remove with a slotted spoon.

Carefully fill a stainless-steel or cast-iron fondue pot with the oil until no more than two-thirds full (to prevent the hot oil from splattering). Keep the oil hot over medium–high heat.

Serves 6

FOR DIPPING

[SEE RECIPES ON FOLLOWING PAGE]

CRUMBED STUFFED OLIVES
BEEF WELLINGTON CROUTES
CHICKEN AND CAPER SKEWERS
SCALLOPS IN PROSCIUTTO

SPINACH AND HERB SALAD WITH TRUFFLE OIL DRESSING

This simple salad of green leaves and fresh herbs provides the perfect counterbalance to the richness of the fondues.

100 g baby spinach leaves
100 g mizuna or baby rocket
2 handfuls basil leaves
2 handfuls mint leaves
1 small handful tarragon leaves

Truffle oil dressing
60 ml (¼ cup) truffle oil
60 ml (¼ cup) lemon juice
1 tablespoon brown sugar

Toss the salad leaves and herbs in a serving bowl. Whisk together the truffle oil, lemon juice and sugar in a small bowl.

To serve, pour the dressing over the salad and toss to combine.

Serves 6

FOR DIPPING

CRUMBED STUFFED OLIVES

18 large feta-stuffed green olives
50 g (½ cup) dried breadcrumbs
4 small red chillies, seeded and finely chopped
2 tablespoons plain flour
1 egg, lightly beaten

Pat the olives dry with paper towel. Combine the breadcrumbs and chilli in a bowl.

Dust the bottom half of each olive with flour, shaking off the excess. Lightly coat with egg and the chilli breadcrumbs. Place on a tray and refrigerate for at least 30 minutes.

Using a long skewer or fondue fork, carefully cook the crumbed olives in the hot oil, in batches, for 1–2 minutes or until golden and crisp.

Serves 6

BEEF WELLINGTON CROUTES

1 tablespoon truffle oil
400 g eye fillet
salt and freshly ground black pepper
1 baguette, ends trimmed, cut into 6 pieces
100 g pate
horseradish, to serve

Rub the truffle oil all over the beef and season well with salt and pepper. Tie with kitchen string to keep the round shape.

Heat a large frying pan over high heat. Cook the beef for 2–3 minutes on each side until seared all over. Remove from the heat and set aside to cool completely, then slice into 6 pieces.

Cut each piece of baguette in half lengthways. Using a long fondue fork, cook the croutes in the hot oil for 1–2 minutes or until golden and crisp.

Spread the pate over the base of the croute then add a slice of beef. Sandwich together with top of croute and use a toothpick to secure. Serve with horseradish.

Makes 6

CHICKEN AND CAPER SKEWERS

2 tablespoons capers, finely chopped
1 clove garlic, finely chopped
2 tablespoons finely chopped parsley
finely grated zest of 1 lemon
12 chicken tenderloins
12 large sage leaves

Combine the capers, garlic, parsley and lemon zest in a bowl.

Using a small sharp knife, cut down one side of each piece of chicken to form a pocket, taking care not to cut all the way through. Fill each pocket with the caper mixture and lay a sage leaf on top of the tenderloin. Starting at the thick end, thread the chicken onto a bamboo skewer, sealing the pocket edge.

Cook the chicken skewers in the hot oil, in batches, for 2–3 minutes or until golden and cooked through.

Makes 12

SCALLOPS IN PROSCIUTTO

12 scallops, roe removed
1 tablespoon olive oil
sea salt and freshly ground black pepper
12 coriander leaves
6 slices parma prosciutto, cut in half lengthways

Rub the scallops with oil and season well with salt and pepper. Lay a coriander leaf on each scallop. Wrap in prosciutto and secure with a toothpick.

Using a long skewer or fondue fork, carefully cook the scallops in the hot oil for 1 minute or until golden.

Makes 12

DARK CHOCOLATE SICHUAN FONDUE

For dessert, spoil your guests with two sweet fondues: velvety dark chocolate with a peppery bite and creamy white chocolate with fragrant rose.

300 ml cream
1½ tablespoons Sichuan peppercorns, toasted
250 g good-quality dark chocolate, roughly chopped
6 drops Tabasco sauce

Place the cream and peppercorns in a saucepan and heat until just at simmering point. Remove from the heat and set aside for 10 minutes to allow the flavours to infuse.

Strain the cream into a clean saucepan. Reheat. Add the chocolate and stir until melted and smooth, then stir through the Tabasco.

Transfer to a fondue pot and keep warm over low heat.

Serves 6

WHITE CHOCOLATE ROSEWATER FONDUE

125 ml (½ cup) cream
2 teaspoons rosewater syrup (available from good delis)
250 g good-quality white chocolate, roughly chopped
½ small handful dried rose petals

Place the cream and rosewater syrup in a saucepan and heat over medium. Add the chocolate and stir until melted and smooth.

Transfer to a fondue pot and keep warm over low heat. Stir through rose petals just before serving.

Serves 6

FOR DIPPING

1 × 250 G BOX TURKISH DELIGHT
3 RIPE FIGS, QUARTERED
HONEYCOMB (SEE RECIPE BELOW)

HONEYCOMB

220 g (1 cup) caster sugar
90 g (¼ cup) golden syrup
1 teaspoon bicarbonate of soda

Grease a 15 cm × 15 cm slice tin and line with baking paper.

Combine the sugar, syrup and 60 ml (¼ cup) of water in a medium saucepan. Cook, stirring constantly, over low heat until the sugar has dissolved. Bring to the boil, then reduce the heat to low and simmer for 10–15 minutes without stirring. Allow the syrup to froth a little and begin to brown, but be careful not to let it burn. The mixture is ready when it reaches 'hard ball' stage. To test, drop ½ teaspoon of syrup into a saucer of cold water and roll to form a firm ball.

Remove the saucepan from the heat and quickly add the bicarbonate of soda, stirring until the mixture is well combined and frothing.

Pour the honeycomb into the prepared tin. Stand for 2 hours or until cooled to room temperature. (Do not refrigerate or the honeycomb will break down.)

Break the honeycomb into pieces, to serve.

Serves 6

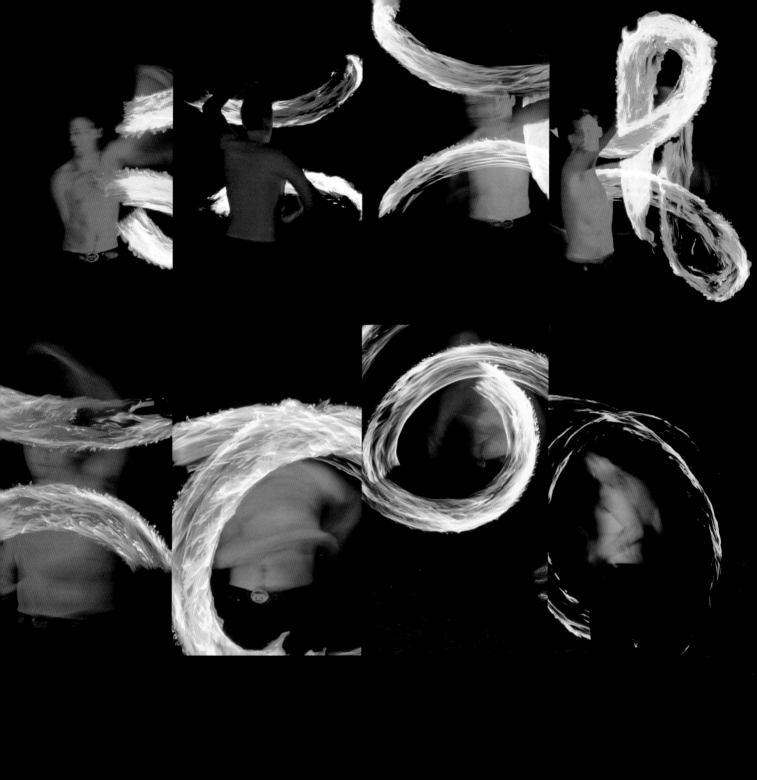

If the title of this book were truly to reflect all the people who made it possible, it would stretch much longer than 'Food, Fashion, Friends'. For a start, there are the 'Friends of Friends', a motley group who sometimes had to dress up in the most unsuitable of outfits in the most inhospitable of settings because one of my mates convinced them it would be fun. Then there are the many friends featured through these pages that knew it was unlikely to be fun but came anyway. Thank you. There are the 'Mystified Colleagues', who found themselves organising food shoots at the same time as assembling fashion collections. Then there are the 'Cast and Crew', the hairdressers, make-up artists, models, photographers, chefs, lighting specialists, handymen, publicists, balloon blower-uppers, animal handlers, glasshouse owners, park rangers, sail purveyors, graffiti artists and cloud-makers who all, in their most individual of ways, played their part. Suffice to say, I could not have done it without them. Nowhere near.

Of the 'Mystified Colleagues,' none was confronted with a wider and weirder array of challenges than my PA Dani Butchart. From trudging across fields with angry bulls looking on menacingly to overseeing the inflation of a thousand balloons, from staying in dodgy country hotels with fights unfolding below her bedroom window to repeatedly having to manoeuvre an antique Indian bed on and off a rain-swept beach involving two staircases, and several 3 a.m. wake-up calls, Dani Butchart was truly heroic.

Dani formed the most dynamic of duos with Matt Redwood, our trusty handyman, the ultimate Mister Fix-It, the finder of solutions to what often seemed like insoluble problems, and a brilliant balloon wrangler to boot. And on behalf of Dani, I would like to thank all the interns and student volunteers who did all the thankless jobs with apprehensive but willing smiles.

My staff at Fleur Wood could not have been more supportive, working extra hours and taking on extra responsibilities well beyond the call of duty. Colleagues more used to producing dresses and camis found themselves embroidering napkins, sewing tablecloths, spray-painting chairs, and, more pleasurably, taste-testing menus. They also had to deal with my many absences. So a huge thank you, especially to Natalie Brock, Caroline Ohn, Leni Wee, Kyoko Tasaka and Andrea Rembeck.

Much of that time away from the studio was spent in the company of the lovely and talented Emily McGregor, one of Sydney's most creative and hardworking stylists. From helping to select the right locations to choosing the right clothes, Emily was both a huge influence and a godsend.

So, too, have been my dear friends Brad Ngata and Glenn Chaplin, stretching back over a decade to when I first started my business. They were not only the stars of the Cloud 9 shoot, but the team behind most of the hair-styling throughout the book. Nobody has been more supportive over the years, nor offered more encouragement and loyalty.

On the publishing front, a new one for me, Pippa Mason from Curtis Brown not only proved to be a beautiful model who braved the chills of the Sydney winter to appear in the woodland shoot, but was the must consummate of agents. I could not have asked for a better guide in helping to navigate the world of Australian publishing.

I also have Pippa to thank for formalising my deal with Julie Gibbs, Publishing Director at Lantern and the first lady of lifestyle publishing. Julie had the courage to believe that a fashion designer could make the transition from the design studio to the kitchen, and for that I am very grateful. She also offered a deft hand when it came to deciding upon that always tricky balance between fashion and food.

Julie leads a team of talents at Lantern who all went beyond the call of duty for this book. Daniel New not only helped with the overall design of the book, but joined the happy band of weekenders who descended upon the Southern Highlands for the country picnic shoot, which looks so effortless in these pages but actually involved an incredible amount of hard work. His input was invaluable. Megan Pigott gracefully helped coordinate all the shoots, Evi Oetomo brought her keen eye for lay-out and design with dedication and enthusiasm, Ariane Durkin expertly edited the text and kept me to schedule, and Ingrid Ohlsson was a wonderful guide to the whole process. My thanks to you all.

This book would not have been without my dear friend Edwina Johnson, a mainstay of the Sydney books scene herself, who suggested I talk to Curtis Brown, and who always thought that the book would find a home at Lantern.

The team at Lantern would not have had much to work with without the beautiful shots of our photographers, Pierre Toussaint, Adrian Lander, Anthony Ong, Kane Skennar, Jordan Graham, Anson Smart, Nerida McMurray. Thank you all for working in the most trying of conditions. Thanks also to their agents Company One, Vivien's Creative and 2C. Many of the models on whom they trained their lenses came from Vivien's Models, Chic Model Management, Priscilla's Model Management – thank you girls. And a big thanks to the agencies for being so supportive of this project. A special thanks to Richard at Sun Studios who often helped provide the right backdrop and all-important equipment.

acknowledgements

Throughout the making of this book, we benefited from the help of a number of corporate sponsors. MAC Cosmetics often sponsored the make-up artist. Princess Cupcake provided the birthday cake for Bonnie. Art of Ice provided the wonderful swan sculpture. Nicola and Andrew from Grandma Takes A Trip, Sydney's best vintage store, leant lots of props and inspiring clothes for the shoots. Thank you for being so generous and supportive. My darling friends, Mark, Maria and Sal, who along with The Beauty Room run Deco Diva, provided dinner sets, glasses and tea sets including a $3000 teapot at a moment's notice. Another friend, Richard Unsworth from Garden Life, provided the plants and shrubbery for the front cover. He also put us in touch with Alpine Nurseries and introduced us to Graham from Garden Gate Nursery who ever so generously allowed us to shoot in his greenhouse where we ran amok for the hot-house tea. Thanks also to Stoneleigh Gallery for the life-like flora and botanicals used on the cover.

Locations were not always easy to find. Especially ones that would allow all our antics. Thank you to Centennial Parklands, the Gaelic Club and a special thanks to the dairy farmers in Robertson, Brian and Amirun McEvilly and their son Bryant, who allowed us to decorate their trees and shoot their prize-winning heifer.

Friends and family leant a variety of props. My mum handed over her finest bone china and gold dinner set on numerous occasions. Sue Bath, our over-worked cleaner, leant her best family heirlooms for the kids shoot. Kat Vidovic and Rob Laurie let us borrow their dog, Betty, for the day and offered great encouragement and enthusiasm. Thanks to the exuberant group of kids who came to Bonnie's birthday, along with their mothers and fathers for dealing with the sugar-highs afterwards. Many darling friends gave up a Saturday to be dressed in outrageous costumes for a shoot that sadly ended up not appearing in the book. A huge thank you to them, too.

The book comes with a soundtrack, and it was put together, with his usual ear for unusual musical combinations, by Gary Sinclair from Tactile Music. He's the prince of the brilliant playlist. Matt Gilmore was our last minute 'ring in' set decorator for Bonnie's Birthday, as well as the Cloud 9 shoot. As ever, Marie-Claude Mallat and Cat Rose from Marie-Claude Mallat Public Relations handled publicity with their usual aplomb and went the extra mile on numerous occasions.

Stylists Lena Bord, Kristine Duran-Thiessen and Michelle Cranston all helped bring my vision alive. Thanks, as well, to Romy Frydman for years of brilliant styling.

On the food front, Peta Dent was a real trooper, coming up with incredible recipes and showing enormous patience managing my learning curve. She was a joy to work with. Thanks also to Adelaide Harris and Mandy Sinclair. Elsewhere in the book, some of the most scrumptious food came from one of Sydney's most scrumptious restaurants, Vini in Surry Hills. Its head chef Dan Johnston and its owner Andrew Cibej were also a joy and very generous.

The celebrity chef Matt Moran was a genuine star. Along with his beautiful wife, Sarah, Matt hosted the most memorable of dinners at which he provided the food, wrote all the recipes and even brought along their gorgeous friends – and all for no charge. As well as being one of Australia's most talented chefs, he is also one of the most generous. Australia's finest jeweller, Julian from J. Farren-Price, lent us close to $1 million worth of jewels to add some 'bling' to the shoot, which it certainly did.

The same is true of all my other friends who have offered help and support. From being human props themselves to supplying friends as human props, whatever the time and whatever the location, they have all been troopers. I would especially like to thank Kristina Ammitzboll, a great friend and creative collaborator who truly saw my vision and helped me to realise it. And Schaan Anderson, my best friend from high school and a constant throughout. Thank you for agreeing to appear on the front cover with me.

I have been very blessed with many wonderful teachers, mentors and healers through my life and would like to thank a few of them now: Siobhan Miriam Cruise, Carlos Raimundo, Grace Gideon, Diane Aigaki, Peter Bablis, Carmel Ehrenkreutz. This dream would not have happened without you all.

My thanks to Mum for her love, support and encouragement. And Dad, I know how proud you would be. I just wish you were here to enjoy these desserts.

Lastly, and most importantly, I must thank my ultimate dining companion, my husband Nick Bryant, whose twin talents as wordsmith and taste-tester proved invaluable. I simply could not have asked for more love or support throughout the creation of this book from its conception to publication. Thank you, darling.

index

LANTERN

Published by the Penguin Group
Penguin Group (Australia)
250 Camberwell Road, Camberwell, Victoria 3124, Australia
(a division of Pearson Australia Group Pty Ltd)
Penguin Group (USA) Inc.
375 Hudson Street, New York, New York 10014, USA
Penguin Group (Canada)
90 Eglinton Avenue East, Suite 700, Toronto, Canada ON M4P 2Y3
(a division of Pearson Penguin Canada Inc.)
Penguin Books Ltd
80 Strand, London WC2R 0RL England
Penguin Ireland
25 St Stephen's Green, Dublin 2, Ireland
(a division of Penguin Books Ltd)
Penguin Books India Pvt Ltd
11 Community Centre, Panchsheel Park, New Delhi – 110 017, India
Penguin Group (NZ)
67 Apollo Drive, Rosedale, North Shore 0632, New Zealand
(a division of Pearson New Zealand Ltd)
Penguin Books (South Africa) (Pty) Ltd
24 Sturdee Avenue, Rosebank, Johannesburg 2196, South Africa

Penguin Books Ltd, Registered Offices: 80 Strand, London, WC2R 0RL, England

First published by Penguin Books Australia Ltd, 2010

1 3 5 7 9 10 8 6 4 2

Text copyright © Fleur Wood 2010. Recipe text © Peta Dent (pp11–18; 81–86; 122–126;
169–181; 204 Honeycomb); Matthew Moran (pp 35–45); Adelaide Harris (pp61–65);
Daniel Johnston (pp100–105; 142–149); Mandy Sinclair (pp198–204).

Photographs copyright © Jordan Graham (ppviii–11; 14; 17–18; 20–21; 52–63; 66–67; 90–100; 102–103;
105; 106–109); Adrian Lander (pp13; 15–16; 19; 48–51; 57; 64–65; 80; 83–84; 87; 101; 104; 124; 143–144;
147–148; 166; 170–171; 176–177; 181; 197; 199–200; 202; 205); Nerida McMurray (pp132–142; 145–146;
149–153); Anthony Ong (ppi; 110–123; 125–131; 154–165; 168–170; 172–176; 178–180; 182; 210);
Kane Skennar (ppvi; 22–32; 35; 45–47; 68–78; 81–82; 85–86; 89); Anson Smart (pp34; 39–44);
Pierre Toussaint (pp184–198; 201–204; 206–209; 212).
The moral right of the author has been asserted.

Designed by Evi O © Penguin Group (Australia)
Cover photograph by Anthony Ong
Typeset in Univers 8.5/10.2pt by Post Pre-Press Group
Colour reproduction by Splitting Image Colour Studio, Pty Ltd, Clayton, Victoria
Printed and bound in China by 1010 Printing International Limited

National Library of Australia
Cataloguing-in-Publication data:

Wood, Fleur.
Food, fashion, friends / Fleur Wood.
9781921382277 (hbk.)
Includes index.
Cookery.
Entertaining.

641.5

penguin.com.au/lantern